Clever Crafts
TO DECORATE YOUR HOME

CHARTWELL
BOOKS, INC.

EDITORIAL
Craft Editor: Tonia Todman
Managing Editor: Judy Poulos
Editorial Coordinators: Rachel Blackmore,
Margaret Kelly
Craft Assistants: Martina Oprey, Paula
McPhail, Dianne Skarratt, Susie Ting, Morag
Robinson, Sherri McLean

DESIGN AND PRODUCTION
Managers: Sheridan Carter, Nadia Sbisa
Layout: Lulu Dougherty, Margie Mulray
Finished Art: Chris Hatcher,
Steven Joseph
Illustrations: Margaret Metcalfe
Photography: Andrew Elton, Harm Mol, David
Young, Vantuan, Murray Cummings
Cover design: Frank Pithers
Cover styling: Tonia Todman

Published by Chartwell Books, Inc.
A division of BOOKSALES, INC.
110 Enterprise Avenue
Secaucus, New Jersey 07094

Some of the contents of this book have
been previously published in other
J.B. Fairfax Press publications.
All care has been taken to ensure the
accuracy of the information in this book but no
responsibility is accepted for any errors or
omissions.

CLEVER CRAFTS TO DECORATE YOUR
HOME
Includes Index
ISBN 1-55521-851-2

Formatted by J.B. Fairfax Press Pty Limited
Printed by Toppan Printing Co, Singapore

PRINTED IN SINGAPORE

Contents

Country
Charm

*T*hese traditional, homely crafts
will bring joy and a whimsical touch
to your home. There are cats for the
doorstep and for your breakfast table,
simple ways with crazy patchwork
and a welcoming topiary tree covered
with pretty dried flowers.

Down to DETAIL

Stenciling

Stenciling is an old and lovely craft with many applications. It is the process of applying paint through a cut-out design. Stencils can be used on tablecloths, sheets, pillowcases, walls, furniture, clothing – the list is virtually endless.

Before You Begin

❏ Stenciling fabric is usually easier if you use a pure cotton. As the finish in some fabrics repels paint, wash your fabric thoroughly before applying any paint.

❏ For cutting out a stencil, use firm, clear plastic sheeting, such as acetate or Mylar®, or sheets of thick Manilla cardboard, coated with a mixture of 50 per cent turpentine and 50 per cent boiled linseed oil. Hang sheets up to dry and wipe thoroughly before using.

❏ Experiment first on scraps for fabric absorption and color strength. Don't judge a color until it is dry. To heat-seal colors, iron the back when dry or use a very hot hair dryer on the paint surface.

❏ Choose a paint that is appropriate for the surface you are stenciling. If working on wood, select a quick-drying paint with only a little water.

❏ If repeating a pattern, for example around a wall or across fabric, measure out each position before painting. Reposition the stencil accurately each time.

❏ Use masking tape to hold the stencil in place while you are painting. Be sure to keep tape clear of area to be stenciled.

❏ Stencil brushes are flat and thick, with a level "surface", because the best way of applying paint is by tapping the brush down onto the space to be painted. Brush strokes can blur the outlines. Before painting, remove excess paint from the brush with a rag.

METHOD
See stencil designs on Pull Out Pattern Sheet at back of book.

1 Place stencil sheet over motif to be copied and trace around design, or trace off design and transfer to cardboard. Cut stencils out using sharp knife.

2 Define stencil areas that will be the same color by covering all other areas with masking tape. Continue to do this until whole stencil has been colored.

3 Taking care to paint the elements in the logical order (main color first then details), start painting from the outside, gradually filling in the entire area until you are happy with the depth of color.

Above left: Applying paint through the stencil
Above: Chair before stenciling
Left: Finished chair

6

It is easy to isolate any part of a stencil to use on its own, or to repeat it to build up the total design. For very simple stencils, use only one color, or one main color and a very small amount of a second one. This makes stenciling simple indeed.

See instructions for making these simple drapes on page 51.

GLUES USED IN THIS BOOK

The variety of glues available throughout the world is extensive. We have used three different types of glue.

1 A glue gun, into which you insert pellets of hardened glue which are then expelled in a hot, melted form. This glue dries very quickly.

2 White glue [PVA (polyvinyl acetate) adhesive], available under numerous brand names. It is milky in appearance, dries clear and shiny and is non-toxic.

3 Spray-adhesive. It is usually ozone friendly, but the fumes make it advisable to use it in a well-ventilated room. It dries quickly and allows for the item to be repositioned.

Country Cat Door Stopper

A welcoming country cat at your door – why not? These happy feline friends are so simple to make you can sew one for every room. If you replace the brick with stuffing, it makes a charming toy.

Before You Begin

❏ If the toy is for a child under three years, embroider all the features.

MATERIALS
- ☐ 16 x 45-in.-piece firm cotton fabric
- ☐ 14 x 21-in.-piece quilter's batting
- ☐ synthetic stuffing
- ☐ house brick
- ☐ pair safety eyes
- ☐ embroidery floss for facial features
- ☐ embroidery floss for whiskers
- ☐ 16 ins. of 1-in.-wide ribbon (or a self-fabric tie) for neck bow
- ☐ small bell
- ☐ craft glue

METHOD

Pattern Outline: ━━ ·· ━━ ·· ━━ ·· ━━
See Pull Out Pattern Sheet at back of book. Neaten all exposed raw edges. $\frac{1}{2}$-in. seams allowed.

1 Place legs, head and tail pieces together in pairs, right sides facing. Stitch together, leaving opening for stuffing at chin and at straight, short edges on legs and tail. Clip curves, turn and iron.

2 Stuff with synthetic stuffing. Hand-stitch head opening. Turn $\frac{1}{2}$ in. along open edge of legs and tail to wrong side.

3 Make darts in body pieces. Place body pieces together with right sides facing and stitch around side and top edges. Turn to right side and iron. Wrap brick in batting and place inside body piece. Fold in edges neatly under brick and hand-stitch to secure. Hand-stitch legs and tail into place.

4 Attach safety eyes following manufacturer's instructions, or embroider eyes, nose and mouth.

5 Thread $3\frac{1}{2}$ in.-lengths of dental floss or several strands of embroidery floss, stiffened with glue, through nose at markings for whiskers. Knot close to fabric to secure. Tie ribbon or self-fabric tie into bow. Hand-stitch just below chin. Stitch bell securely in place.

Country Cat Place Mat

Make one of these delightful breakfast companions for everyone in your family. For an added dash of fun, make each one in a different, but toning, country print.

Before You Begin

❏ Cut out the place mat following the pattern on the Pattern Sheet for the Country Cat Door Stopper (page 8) but cutting the place mat 13 x 10 ins.

MATERIALS
For each place mat:
☐ tracing paper and pencil
☐ 10 ins. of 45-in.-wide country print cotton fabric
☐ 10 ins. fine synthetic batting
☐ embroidery floss
☐ matching sewing threads
☐ clear-drying craft glue

METHOD
See Pull Out Pattern Sheet at back of book. ¹/₄-in.-seams allowed.

1 Trace off pattern for cat's body, head and legs from Pattern Sheet.

2 Using tracing as your pattern, cut two bodies, two tails, two heads and four legs from fabric, and one body, one tail, one head and two legs from batting.

3 Pin batting to wrong side of one head, one tail and two legs. Place remaining fabric pieces on pinned pieces with right sides together and raw edges even. Stitch around outside edges, leaving an opening for turning. Trim seams to eliminate bulk and clip corners for ease. Turn and iron. Hand-stitch openings closed.

4 Pin batting to wrong side of one body piece. Quilt body piece in diagonal rows using a quilting guide, if you have one, or following evenly spaced lines of masking tape.

5 Place legs and then tail on body, overlapped as shown. Trim away any of leg that shows beyond tail and eliminate bulk wherever possible. Topstitch legs and tail in place, stitching ¹/₄ in. from edge.

6 Topstitch around head ¹/₄ in. from edge. Embroider facial features. Eyes and mouth are done in tiny chain stitches and mouth is satin stitch. Make whiskers from strands of light-colored embroidery floss, stiffened with craft glue. Stitch whiskers through from one side of nose to other, making a tiny knot on either side to secure strands. Cut whiskers to an appropriate length.

7 Place remaining body piece on top of trimmed piece with right sides together and raw edges even. Stitch around outside edge, leaving an opening for turning. Trim seams, turn and iron. Hand-stitch opening closed.

8 Stitch head to body, stitching over line of topstitching.

9 Embroider a bow at neck, using tiny chain stitches in two colors to form stripes. Take care to curve stitches to look like ribbon.

Decoupage Cat Boxes

For the ultimate cat lover, these boxes can hold a variety of treasures including a brush, collar, bells, fluffy balls and toy mice.

MATERIALS
- ☐ firm white paper
- ☐ pencil
- ☐ tracing paper
- ☐ sharp scissors
- ☐ paints or colored felt-tip pens
- ☐ white glue
- ☐ soft paintbrush for gluing
- ☐ suitable boxes
- ☐ clear spray varnish

METHOD

1 Trace cat outlines and color them in with paints or felt-tip pens. Cut out cats with sharp scissors.

2 Experiment with layout of cats on your box until you are happy, then spread glue over area cats will cover. Lay cats on glued surface, then paint another coat of glue over top. Continue placing cats, overlapping if desired, and covering with glue each time.

3 When glue is completely dry, spray with several coats of clear spray varnish.

Crazy Patchwork

This is the easiest patchwork method known! You need a little patience assembling the pieces, but accuracy is not essential to achieve the overall effect! First make up your patchwork fabric, then this cheerful cat teapot cosy and pillow.

Before You Begin

❏ Choose fabrics of the same type and weight to make laundering easier.

❏ Place the fabric pieces together in groups to see how they look side by side and alter the combinations until you are pleased with the effect.

❏ Where fabrics overlap, neaten the edge of the upper one – either by turning it under or by covering it with ribbon or lace. The neatened edge is then laid flat, overlapping the raw edge of the adjoining piece.

Patchwork Fabric

MATERIALS

❏ scraps of coordinating fabrics. These can be combinations of prints, contrasting textures, lace and ribbons, or bright shiny plains and prints.

METHOD

Allow ¹/₂ in. for seams, turnings and hems.

1 Decide on your patchwork pattern. Neaten all visible raw edges as described. Pin or baste pieces together.

2 Stitch through all thicknesses. Continue adding pieces until the required fabric size is achieved. Cut out pattern pieces for your particular project.

Patchwork Pillow

MATERIALS

❏ patchwork square 16 x 16 ins.
❏ 3¹/₂ yds. of 4-in.-wide ruffle
❏ 3¹/₂ yds. of 4-in.-wide lace or 5-yd. strip of 3¹/₂-in.-wide lace fabric, hemmed along one long edge
❏ two pieces backing fabric, each 16 x 8¹/₂ ins.
❏ 12-in.-long zipper
❏ 16 in.-square pillow form

METHOD

Make pillow following directions for Ruffled Piped Pillow on page 40.

1 To make lace-trimmed ruffle: Join short ends of lace and of fabric ruffle strips together. Hem both strips along one long side.

2 Place lace over fabric, matching raw edges. Gather ruffle strip and lace along raw edges, through all thicknesses. Place ruffle around pillow front with right sides facing and raw edges matching. Stitch through all thicknesses.

3 Make pillow back as instructed in Down To Detail on page 42.

Left: Patchwork Pillow
Below: Don't be alarmed if the wrong side of your work looks as messy as this

Cat Teapot Cosy

MATERIALS

- ☐ patchwork fabric rectangle 21 x 14 ins. for front and back
- ☐ 21 x 14 ins. lining
- ☐ 12 ins. of 45-in.-wide coordinating fabric for tail, legs and head
- ☐ synthetic stuffing for tail, legs and head
- ☐ 21 x 14 ins. quilter's batting
- ☐ embroidery floss and safety eyes
- ☐ 16 ins. of 1-in-wide ribbon; small bell
- ☐ craft glue

METHOD

Pattern Outline: ━ ━ ‥ ━ ‥ ━ ‥ ━
See Pull Out Pattern Sheet at back of book. $\frac{1}{2}$-in. seams allowed.

1 Make your Patchwork Fabric as instructed on page 11.

2 Cut out pattern pieces from patchwork fabric as directed. Cut front and back pieces from batting as well.

3 Place leg and tail pieces together in pairs with right sides facing. Stitch around outside edges, leaving short straight edge open. Clip curves, turn to right side and iron.

4 Stuff legs and tail. Take care not to stuff too firmly. Pin opening closed.

5 Place head pieces together with right sides facing and raw edges matching. Stitch around outside, leaving opening for turning at chin. Clip curves and trim angles. Turn to right side and iron. Stuff. Close opening by hand.

6 Place front and back body pieces and body lining pieces together, with right sides facing and raw edges matching.

Stitch around curved edges of body and of lining pieces. Clip curves.

7 Place body and lining together with right sides facing and raw edges around lower edges matching. Stitch around lower edge, leaving a 5-in. gap for turning. Turn through opening, pushing lining up into body. Inside lower edge (on lining side) hand-stitch lining to seam allowance to prevent lining rolling out.

8 Hand-stitch tail and legs firmly into position. Overlap legs slightly at front and hand-stitch to secure.

9 Embroider nose and mouth. Insert eyes following manufacturer's instructions. Stiffen embroidery floss with glue for whiskers. Stitch whiskers on either side of nose; knot close to fabric to secure. Attach bow and bell. Hand-stitch head in place, securing at back and sides.

Topiary Tree

In days past, clever gardeners clipped trees, shrubs and hedges into wonderful shapes. Today the tradition lives on in these versatile, decorative trees you can make yourself – in any size.

Before You Begin

❏ Remember balance is important. Don't put a very tall tree into a small pot.

❏ The trees become quite top-heavy once completed; consider this when securing the tree in its container.

❏ For miniature trees, use small polystyrene foam balls instead of a floral foam block and sharpened wood skewers or dowel for the stem. They look wonderful as table centerpieces for special occasions.

❏ Topiary trees are ideal for special occasions and can be covered with small balloons, leaves or flowers.

MATERIALS
- ☐ assorted ribbons; strips of tulle; decorative fabric; dried flowers and leaves; nuts; shells; seed pods
- ☐ floral foam block or ball
- ☐ nails; tissue paper; paper
- ☐ length of dowel or an attractive branch for stem of tree
- ☐ pot or container
- ☐ spray paint, if desired
- ☐ small quantity of quick-dry cement
- ☐ medium-weight floral wire
- ☐ small wire cutters and pliers

METHOD

1 Hammer nails into sides of one end of stem and sharpen other end.

2 Lay paper across drainage hole in pot and stand nailed end of stem in pot. Fill pot with cement and allow to dry.

3 Wire up all trimmings into bunches and wind wire around stems. Paint any trimmings now. Tie bows or layer ribbon and wire layers together. Strips of tulle and fabric can be used as ribbons.

4 When cement is dry, pull centre of foam block firmly down onto sharpened, top end of stem. Start inserting wired trimmings into foam block, first building up a circular perimeter to act as a guide. This will prevent you subsequently having some bunches too far into or out of the circle. Remember to build up this perimeter from all angles – try to imagine you are creating a smooth, round ball.

5 When all bunches are inserted, scrunch up tissue paper or similar to hide cement and place pot into basket.

6 Rim of pot can be decorated with glued-on nuts, shells, dried flowers or seed pods.

Above: Pushing wired bunches of trimmings into foam ball
Right: Topiary Tree

Terra Cotta Pots

Simple, everyday terra cotta pots are perfect for stenciled or painted trims. The naturally warm tones of the clay work well with a variety of colors in traditional motifs, reminiscent of folk art images.

Before You Begin

❏ Examine the shape and features of your pots for inspiration. Many of them have grooves and lines which lend themselves to painting.

❏ Use both freehand and stencils for painting your pots. Stencils can be bought, or made quite simply from firm, clear plastic sheets.

❏ Don't neglect the inside of your pot. If you plan to use it for a plant holder, then paint just inside the rim. If you want to use it only as a decorative item, you can make the inside just as interesting to look at as the outside.

❏ Painting stencils is quite easy if you follow a couple of simple rules – keep the stencil still and firmly pressed against the side of the pot (masking tape can be useful here) and do not load your brush with too much paint at one time. Stenciling a curved surface can be a bit tricky, but is not impossible if you take it slowly.

❏ If you decide to keep your pots indoors, spray them with a clear varnish to preserve and protect the paint and to give your pot a "glow".

MATERIALS
- ☐ sheets of firm, clear plastic
- ☐ fine felt-tip pen
- ☐ sharp craft knife
- ☐ medium round paintbrushes for lines
- ☐ small natural sponges or stencil brushes for stencils
- ☐ acrylic paints
- ☐ old saucers to hold paint

METHOD
See Pull Out Pattern Sheet at back of book for additional designs.

1 To make your stencils: Lay plastic sheet over motif you wish to use and trace outline with fine felt-tip pen.

2 Using sharp craft knife and a cutting board, cut around outline, cutting away those areas you wish paint to cover.

3 Make sure your pots are clean and free of dust or grit. Place stencil in desired position against pot and fill in color using a sponge or stencil brush.

4 Paint in any lines and grooves with the round brush.

14

Down to DETAIL

Folk Art Stool

The folk art tradition began in the 15th and 16th centuries when ordinary folk began to imitate the fine painted furniture and decorations they saw in their churches and the homes of the gentry. Naturally, the style and subjects of the painting have not remained static in all those years and differing regional styles have also developed.

Apart from linen cupboards, tables and chairs, folk artists painted dowry chests and storage boxes. One family treasure, the "bride's box", was usually painted with a loving-couple motif, often surrounded by a romantic saying.

MATERIALS
☐ lidded stool in raw wood
☐ wet and dry sandpaper, 240 and 120
☐ tracing paper
☐ carbon paper
☐ pencil and ruler
☐ Roymac series 2800, flat brush size 8
☐ Rowney S40, round brush size 3
☐ brush for applying polyurethane varnish
☐ Matisse Water-Based Clear Sealer
☐ polyurethane varnish, oil-based
☐ Matisse Professional Artists' Acrylic Background Paint: AB Antique Blue
☐ Matisse Professional Artists' Acrylic Colors (Flow formula): AW Antique White, T Terra Cotta, P Pink (T + AW), YO Yellow Oxide, MB Mars Black, G Green (Y + MB)
☐ Matisse Oil Patina, BU Burnt Umber
☐ soft cotton cloth

METHOD
See Pull Out Pattern Sheet at back of book for additional designs.

1 Sand stool with 240 and then 120 grade sandpaper. Seal with Matisse Water-Based Clear Sealer, following manufacturer's instructions. Allow to dry.

2 Rule a pencil line 1 1/2 ins. in from each edge on top and long sides of stool. Paint one coat of AB around these marked panels, sides and inside legs. Allow to dry.

Raw wood stool – sanded and ready to paint

3 Mix a dark green paint color with the round brush and paint an 1/8-in. line around inner edge of panels and 3/4 in. inside edge of stool ends. Allow to dry.

Measure up and draw in panels for top and sides

Sanding the edges of the stool

4 With 120 grade sandpaper, dipped in clean water, sand lightly on edges and corners of stool where normal wear patches might appear. Wipe off scrubbings with a clean, damp, cotton cloth as you go.

Above: Transferring the oval design
Right: Folk art painting can be used to decorate many different objects

5 Trace in inner and outer outlines of oval-shape for stool lid and transfer them to center of stool top. Paint them in a dark mix of G. Allow to dry, then draw in flowers and leaves.

6 Paint leaves over dark G oval in a medium G. Paint S strokes of leaves with a shading of YO on inside and MB on outside. Paint in flowers, following Painting Flowers guide below. Allow to dry.

Painting the side panel

7 Trace floral design for sides of stool. Transfer designs to stool. Paint in leaves, stems and calyxes, using medium G and round brush. Paint in flowers following Painting Flowers guide below. Allow to dry.

Adding the antique finish

8 Leave painting to dry for a day or so. Make a pad or wad with a soft cloth and place a line of BU about ¹/₂ in. long on it. Wipe evenly over entire stool with pad,

adding another ¹/₂-in. line of BU as necessary. Wipe back colour to desired depth, leaving it darker at edges and lighter in centers. Allow to dry completely. Drying time will depend on thickness of oil patina and degree of humidity.

9 Apply several coats of polyurethane varnish, allowing each coat to dry before applying next coat.

PAINTING FLOWERS

Roses
Using round brush and T, paint a large circle and one comma petal on dark side. Mix T and G and paint a dark hollow in mouth of rose, blending in top edge to soften line. Load brush with P, then dip it into fresh AW. Starting at mid-front of rose, under hollow, press point of brush down so colors blend and make a comma stroke by lifting brush slowly as you follow edge of hollow up and around. Make another comma under first one. Repeat for other side of rose, varying amount of white as shown. Paint three more commas under bowl of rose in same way.

Blue flowers
Load brush with AB and then dip it into fresh AW. For each petal, paint one curved stroke to left and another to right giving a variegated color. Center is a circle of T with a highlight of YO.

Yellow flowers
These are painted in same way as blue flowers, using YO and AW. Center is T with a shadow of dark G.

S Stroke

Comma Stroke

Flower painting design for sides of stool

Fabric Fantasy

Fabrics set the decorating scheme, and the choice is endless. Color, texture and pattern are the integral elements to watch for, but the hardest part is deciding which one to choose.

Decorating with Decoupage

Decoupage is about covering almost any flat or gently curving surface with paper cutouts. Traditionally it involves varnish, sandpaper – and lots of effort! In our clever version, white glue replaces the old materials and most of the hard work!

Before You Begin

❏ Gather up as much decoupage material as you think you will need and have all the pieces cut out before you begin. You can add more later but you'll need a reasonable supply to begin with.

❏ Plan the design you wish to achieve before you start gluing. Experiment with colors and the distribution of motifs.

❏ If you wish to cover the item completely, use a layer of background paper pieces first. Cut these small shapes at random and overlap them to completely cover the item. Glue the decorative motifs on as the next layer.

❏ Items covered with glue, once completely dried, may be wiped clean with a damp cloth, but never immersed in water.

MATERIALS
❏ white glue
❏ soft brush for applying glue
❏ pieces of wallpaper; wrapping paper; greeting cards; magazine clippings etc
❏ objects to be covered, such as tins; trays; place mats; papier-mache shapes; terra cotta pots etc
❏ small sharp scissors for cutting paper

METHOD

1 Cut out motifs from paper precisely or leave a ¼-in. margin around motif.

2 Begin placing motifs according to your design by coating a small area with undiluted glue and placing cutout motif onto glued area. Once it is in place, coat motif with glue.

3 Repeat this process until design is completed. Allow to dry, then coat with glue again. For a deep shine repeat this last step.

Pillow *Talk*

*T*hese soft surprises will delight you. Pillows on beds, sofas and chairs add luxury and comfort, and can bring a fresh new look to any setting. You'll also find out how to make a traditional feather-filled bed quilt.

Embroidered Accessories

Delicate pansies in simple cross stitch give real charm to pillow-cases and tiebacks, adding gentleness to your private retreat.

MATERIALS

- ☐ 20 ins. of 5-in.-wide 14 count white Aida for pillowcases and 22 x 9 ins. for each tieback
- ☐ 1 pair plain white, ruffled pillowcases
- ☐ 32 ins. of white cotton fabric for tieback backing
- ☐ narrow white satin ribbon
- ☐ DMC Stranded Cotton, 1 skein each: Dark Green 936; Medium Green 3347; Light Blue 800; Dark Blue 311; Pale Blue 775; Medium Blue 334
- ☐ ³/₄-in.-wide white lace edging

Pillow Sham

METHOD

See page 28 for embroidery graph and key.

1 To prepare Aida, count five squares down from top, seven squares up from bottom and fourteen squares in from both sides and baste along these rows with contrasting colored thread as a guide for hemming.

2 To commence sewing, find and mark center of Aida by folding widthwise and lengthwise. Count fifteen squares down from basted line and work your cross stitch following design graph and key.

3 Keep repeating pattern along length of Aida by counting down five squares from bottom stitch of completed design. Leave five squares between each pattern.

4 When pattern is completed, backstitch around flowers, using a single strand of 311 and, where indicated by a half cross, backstitches of 936.

5 When stitching is finished, fold Aida along basted lines to mark hems. Pin lace edging under folded edges and stitch in place.

6 Pin Aida onto pillowcase and stitch into place by hand or machine.

Tieback

METHOD

Pattern Outline: ....
See Pull Out Pattern Sheet at back of book.

1 Trace pattern and cut two Tiebacks from Aida. Fold Aida fabric widthwise and lengthwise to find and mark center. Center first motif over this point.

2 Because of Tieback shape, the two outer designs must be stepped. For left-hand motif, count up ten squares from green at bottom of center design. Count one square up for right-hand design.

3 Sew lace edging around right side of each Tieback with right sides facing and raw edges even.

4 Cut out two backing pieces, using Tieback pattern. Place backing and embroidered pieces together with right sides facing. Stitch around outside edge, leaving an opening for turning. Turn to right side and iron. Sew ribbon to ends of Tieback to secure it to a wall hook.

Embroidered curtain Tieback and Pillow Sham add old-world charm to a bedroom

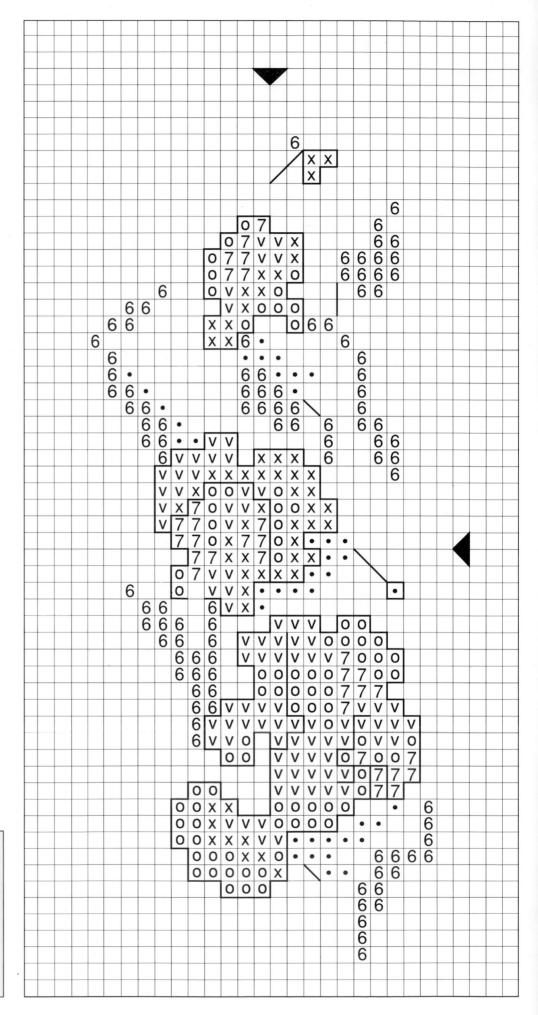

KEY

	DMC	Color
6	936	Dark Green
•	3347	Medium Green
X	800	Light Blue
7	311	Dark Blue
V	775	Pale Blue
O	334	Medium Blue
Cross stitch	2 strands	
Backstitch	1 strand	

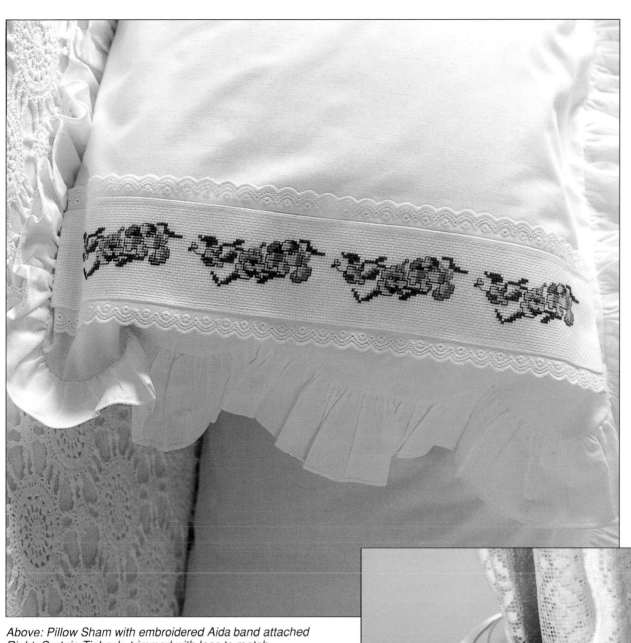

Above: Pillow Sham with embroidered Aida band attached
Right: Curtain Tieback, trimmed with lace to match
Pillow Sham
Left: Embroidery graph for pansy designs

Bedroom Set

Filling your bedroom with the dazzling beauty and romance of English roses, these coordinates are just what decorating dreams are made of.

The Bedspread and Lamp Shade adapt a 17th and 18th century technique called broderie perse, a type of applique in which motifs are cut from a piece of print fabric and then applied to a larger piece of material. At about this time, printed chintz, imported from India, was very popular in Britain – so popular, in fact, that imports of chintz were banned for a while, in order to protect the local industry. Broderie perse was a means of making a small amount of precious material go a long way.

Bedspread

Before You Begin

❑ The Bedspread was made to fit a standard double bed but can quite easily be adjusted to fit a larger-sized bed by altering the size of the central panel. The best way to ensure a good fit is to draw a diagram for your own bed like the one shown here, marking your own measurements. Following your diagram, calculate the amount of fabric you will need.

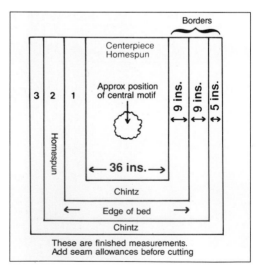

These are finished measurements.
Add seam allowances before cutting

❑ The borders of printed fabric were cut across the width of the fabric and joined to give the correct length. If your fabric has a one-way pattern, mark the top edge of each piece as you cut it and place that edge towards the center panel.

❑ Traditionally, these bedspreads were not quilted. You can quilt yours, if you prefer, by cutting a piece of batting to the size of the complete Bedspread and basting it to the wrong side of the Bedspread before you begin quilting around the motifs. Use a sheet for the backing and bind the edges with a complementary fabric or the plain homespun.

MATERIALS
❑ sufficient print fabric and plain homespun. (We used 4 yds. of print fabric and 4¼ yds. of plain homespun.)
❑ Vliesofix® or Wonder Under*
❑ matching sewing thread

METHOD

1 Draw a diagram for your own Bedspread like the one at left, using your own measurements. Cut out center panel, print and plain panels, following your diagram.

2 After experimenting with possible arrangements, roughly cut out motifs for your applique from remaining print fabric. Iron Vliesofix or alternative to wrong side of motifs and cut out carefully, very close to edge of motifs.

3 Peel off paper backing from motifs for center panel and iron them into place.

4 Stitch on first print border, mitering corners for a neat finish.

5 Sew on first plain border, mitering corners. Prepare and apply applique motifs in same way as for center panel.

6 Sew on outer print border, mitering corners. Hem around outside edge.

Shaped Pillowcase

❏ If the front is to be quilted, the front pieces must be cut out at least 2 ins. larger all around to allow for shrinkage during the quilting process.

MATERIALS
- ☐ 44 ins. fabric for front and ruffle
- ☐ 36 ins. toning fabric for back
- ☐ 36 ins. square batting (if quilting)
- ☐ 36 ins. square fine cotton or home-spun for lining (if quilting)

METHOD
See Pull Out Pattern Sheet at back of book.
Pattern Outline: ─────────────

1 From main fabric, cut one front, three 3-in.-wide strips for ruffle, one back and one flap. If you are quilting front, cut out one front in batting and one in lining as well.

2 Smooth lining on a table, face down. Place batting on top, then main front piece face upwards. Make sure there are no puckers or wrinkles. Pin through all thicknesses using safety pins, or baste layers together. Quilt around motifs by hand or machine. When quilting is completed, recut front to correct size.

3 Join strips for ruffle. Make a narrow hem or overlock along one long edge. Selvages will act as finish on two short ends. Stitch a row of gathering stitches along other long edge. Gather fabric until it measures approximately 2½ yds.

4 Pin ruffle to front with right sides facing and raw edges even, easing in a little extra width on corners A and B. Pin or baste finished edge of ruffle to front, taking care to catch in corners. This will stop ruffle from folding or dropping out of place and from being caught in seams. Take special care at corners C and D to fold end of ruffle back out of way of seamline, as this end of ruffle is not stitched down (see Figure 1).

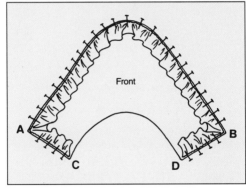

Figure 1

5 Stitch ruffle in place, leaving finished edge pinned or basted until all work is complete.

6 With right sides facing, pin flap to right side of front at one end. This will be open end of pillowcase. Stitch only across end, then open out flap to hang from end as shown by dotted line (see Figure 2).

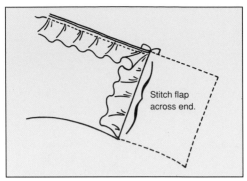

Stitch flap across end.

Figure 2

7 Finish matching end of back with a small hem. Pin back to front with right sides together and pinning all around except where there is a hem.

8 Fold open end of flap back over end of pillow and pin side seams (see Figure 3).

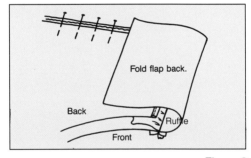

Fold flap back.

Back

Ruffle

Front

Figure 3

9 Stitch around pillowcase, except across end where flap is folded back. Turn whole cover right side out and remove pins or basting. Iron well.

Shaped Pillowcase showing quilting detail

Lamp Shade

❏ Our frame is 44 ins. in diameter at the bottom and is 9 ins. deep; the top is 39 ins. in diameter. Adjust the fabric measurements to fit your shade.

MATERIALS
- ☐ 45 x 12 ins. fabric
- ☐ 2¼ yds. pregathered lace
- ☐ 2¼ yds. braid
- ☐ small amount of narrow ribbon for bow
- ☐ white glue
- ☐ elastic
- ☐ Vliesofix® or Wonder Under®

METHOD

1 Cut out applique motif from fabric, apply Vliesofix or alternative to back and position applique in center of fabric rectangle. Satin stitch around motif.

2 Join fabric short ends with a tapered seam, with piece starting at 44 ins. wide and decreasing to 39 ins.

3 Make an elastic casing at top and bottom. Thread elastic through casing after placing cover over frame. Draw up elastic until cover sits firmly on frame.

4 Glue lace and braid around top and bottom of Lamp Shade. Glue a small bow in center at bottom of applique.

Dust Ruffle

❏ Check the depth of the ruffle required for your own bed, remembering to add about 1 in. for seam allowances. On the illustrated dust ruffle, the finished depth of the ruffle is 14 ins. The cut depth before stitching is approximately 15 ins. This depth of ruffle allows three lengths to be cut from one width of fabric. Measure around the bed, two sides and one end. Double this measurement. This will give the total length of the ruffle. Since you will be able to cut three lengths from the width, divide the total length of the ruffle by three. Add enough for the seam allowance for two joins and the hems for two ends. This will give the amount of fabric required. Our version needed almost 2¼ yds. of fabric for the ruffle.

MATERIALS
- ☐ sufficient fabric for Dust Ruffle
- ☐ sufficient sheeting or homespun for base rectangle
- ☐ matching sewing thread

METHOD

1 Measure top of bed base and, using sheeting or homespun, cut a rectangle to fit this part.

2 Join sections of ruffle to make one long piece. Hem short ends and make a very narrow hem along one long side.

3 Stitch two rows of gathering stitches along other long side, preferably in quarters or even eighths, for ease of working. Pull up gathers evenly to correct length for going around homespun or sheeting rectangle.

4 Sew ruffle to edge of rectangle on three sides.

Lamp Shade with applique trim

33

Down to DETAIL

Log Cabin Quilt

Log cabin is perhaps the most popular of the traditional quilting patterns. The design depends on the contrast between the light and dark fabrics used in each of the quilt blocks. The placement of the light and dark halves of the blocks determines the particular log cabin design.

Before You Begin

❏ In this quilt, the blocks are arranged in the "straight furrow" pattern, where the dark halves are set adjacent to one another in a diagonal line across the quilt.

❏ Traditionally, the log cabin design is a great way of using material scraps left over from other projects. Making a scrap quilt can be quite a challenge but it is also very satisfying. For this quilt, three or four pieces of fabric were purchased to supplement the forty or fifty different scrap fabrics. Some scrap fabrics which did not quite suit the rustic color scheme were dyed in tea to give the right tones. Continuity is maintained by using the same color for the center square of each block. This center square is usually red or yellow, representing the warm fireplace at the center of the cabin.

❏ You can also mix different weights of fabric in a log cabin quilt but, if you intend to wash it, it is best that you use cotton or polyester/cotton. If you are prepared to have it dry-cleaned, you can use velvets, silks and other textured fabrics.

❏ The size of the quilt can be varied by adding or subtracting blocks, by making the center of each block rectangular instead of square or by adding more strips to each block.

❏ Quantities given for fabrics can only be approximate, as the actual amounts needed will depend on the size of your scraps.

❏ Always collect more scrap pieces than you think you will need to give you the greatest scope in arranging the colors. In this quilt, there are no two blocks which are identical and no fabric is repeated in the same block.

❏ When joining your blocks and rows, it is important to keep the seam allowances constant, the seams aligned and all the angles square. If you fail to do this, the blocks will be distorted and your quilt will not come together neatly.

Size: approximately 55 x 63 ins.
Total number of blocks: 42, set 6 x 7

MATERIALS
☐ approximately 49 ins. light fabrics
☐ approximately 70 ins. dark fabrics
☐ 10 ins. red or yellow fabric for centers
☐ 40 ins. total of scraps or one fabric for borders
☐ 55 x 63 ins. batting
☐ 55 x 63 ins. backing fabric
☐ Olfa cutter and mat
☐ pins
☐ matching sewing thread

METHOD
$1/4$-in. seams allowed.

To piece quilt top

1 Cut all fabrics into strips approximately $1^1/2$ ins. wide. Using an Olfa cutter, you can cut many layers at same time. Cut $2^1/2$-in.-wide strips, then cut into $2^1/2$-in. squares for center of each block.

2 Group all fabrics into three piles – one light, one dark and all center squares.

3 Take a pile of center squares and chainsew them, right sides together, to edge of a light strip. Cut squares apart, even with edge of center square. Iron seams away from center square.

4 Stitch a light strip at right angles to strip just sewn. Cut and iron. One light round is now complete.

5 Stitch a dark strip to edge of center square, placing it at right angles to strip just attached. Cut and iron.

6 Attach another dark strip to fourth side of center square in same way. Cut and iron. One whole round is now complete.

7 Continue attaching strips, light on one side and dark on other, for three full rounds. Make 42 blocks in same way.

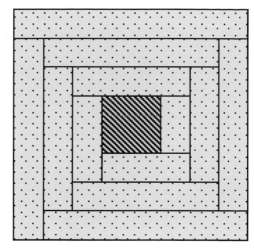

Complete Block

To assemble

1 The best way to assemble your quilt top is to lay all blocks on a flat surface (your floor is ideal) in "straight furrow" style (see Figure 1).

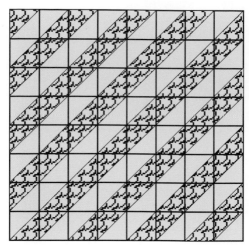

Figure 1

2 Join blocks together horizontally in seven rows of six blocks (see Figure 2).

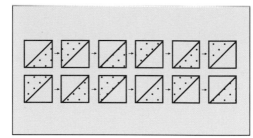

Figure 2

3 Join rows together to form quilt top (see Figure 3).

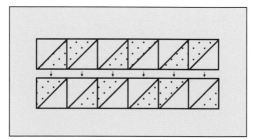

Figure 3

4 If you want to add borders, you can make them by stitching remaining strips together or by cutting appropriate lengths from a toning fabric. To calculate length of side borders, measure length of quilt top. Always measure through quilt center, not down sides. Cut two borders to this length and 4 ins. wide. Join borders to sides of quilt top with right sides together.

5 For top and bottom borders, measure width of quilt top, including side borders, measuring through center. Cut top and bottom borders to this length and 4 ins. wide. Stitch them in place. Iron quilt top well.

To quilt

1 Place complete quilt top face down on a flat surface. Place batting on top and backing fabric on top of that, facing upwards. Secure three layers together with safety pins or by basting.

2 On right side, quilt by stitching in squares as shown or in a pattern of your own. If you prefer, you can tie your quilt with strong cotton at intersection of blocks and in centers of blocks.

3 Cut strips of fabric 4 ins. wide for binding. Measure lengths required in same way as for borders. Fold binding strips over double with wrong sides together. Pin bindings to right side of quilt, first sides and then top and bottom, with raw edges even. Stitch. Turn folded edge to wrong side of quilt and slipstitch in place. Sign and date your quilt.

LOG CABIN QUILTS

Log cabin quilts are ideal for beginners and the pattern can be easily adapted to smaller projects such as pillows, pot holders and place mats. This quilt is a log cabin quilt in the "barn raising" style, one of the most popular patterns. It can be a true scrapbag quilt, utilizing quite small pieces of fabric where the only governing factor is the contrast between light and dark colors.

Like all log cabin quilts, it is based on a pattern of light and dark rectangles, pieced around a center square. The rectangles are laid in such a way as to represent the logs used by the early American settlers to build their cabins. Some early quilts even had a little chimney stitched in to further underline the theme. The center square of the block is often red, to denote the fireplace, or yellow, to represent the lighted window or warm hearth.

These days, most log cabin quilts are made from light and dark printed, dress-weight cottons but, in the past, quilters often used wool as well. Mixing silks, velvets, and other "luxury" fabrics produces a lovely quilt with quite a different feeling about it. Traditional log cabin quilts were made without a border, but this is not a strict rule and these days quilters often add a plain or print border.

While the basic ingredients of a log cabin block remain the same – half in light and half in dark – changing the way in which the rectangles are placed or the blocks are joined will give you quite a different-looking quilt. Joining the blocks so that the dark halves are adjacent to one another and the light halves are adjacent to one another, gives a design of alternating light and dark diamonds. Piecing the

blocks and joining them so that the dark and light halves form alternating diagonals, reminiscent of a roof line, make this design known as "barn raising". Placing the blocks so that the dark and light halves travel diagonally across the quilt creates the pattern known as "straight furrow".

Making a block so that the light and dark quarters are opposite the same quarters and joining the blocks side by side across the row, makes yet another pattern, called "courthouse steps".

Above: A log cabin quilt
Right: A log cabin place mat

Continental Quilt

These feather or down-filled quilts, also called duvets or doonas, are the ideal solution for cold winter nights. They provide the warmth of several blankets without the weight.

Before You Begin

❏ The size of your quilt is entirely up to you. Generally a double bed quilt should be approximately 2¼ x 2¼ yds. and a single bed quilt 2¼ x 1¾ yds.

❏ Use a very closely woven fabric, like japara (not always easy to find), downproof cambric or a very closely woven furnishing chintz or cotton. Don't use sheets – feathers like to work their way through the threads of the fabric and escape!

❏ If joining lengths of fabric to make a single piece use edge-concealing seams such as run-and-fell or French seams.

❏ The choice of filling is up to you. Down is more expensive than feathers, but is warmer, lighter and bulkier. A combination of feathers and down is a good compromise. Synthetic stuffing is suitable for anyone allergic to feathers.

❏ Generally, filling comes in packs by weight. Approximately 3 lbs. of feather-and-down combination filling was needed for our double bed quilt. Synthetic stuffing weighs more than feathers. Experiment until you are happy with the weight and feel of your own quilt.

❏ Tape is used to create channels for the filling. Choose firm cotton twill tape. Bias binding is unsuitable. Quantity of tape will depend on how many channels you make in your quilt. For our double bed quilt, 8-in.-wide channels suited the fabric pattern. This meant that we had 9 rows of tape (giving us 10 channels), so we used 20½ yds. of twill tape. Length of tape required is equal to number of rows of tape x length of quilt cover. Decide on the width of channels best for your fabric.

❏ A feather quilt is, theoretically, washable – but the bulk is daunting when hanging it out to dry. Dry cleaning is effective. Hanging your quilt out regularly to air in the sun will keep it smelling clean and fresh.

❏ Those experienced with feathers-and-down say that one should only work in the bathroom with the door shut! When filling your quilt, place the open bag of feathers in the bath. This helps to confine the fly-away feathers to a relatively draught-free area with little for them to stick to.

❏ Pegging the quilt (at each channel) to a line strung above the bath may help you to fill channels evenly.

MATERIALS
☐ sufficient fabric to cut a front and a back of desired size and allow 4 ins. for turning, all around
☐ sufficient filling of your choice (see Before You Begin)
☐ sufficient 2-in.-wide cotton twill tape (see Before You Begin)

METHOD
1 Turn in 4 ins. all around each quilt piece to mark foldline for hems. Fold quilt and iron along tape lines at decided distances apart. This step is not necessary if you have striped fabric that indicates the channel widths.

2 Stitch one edge of tape along one stripe/crease on the wrong side of one quilt piece. Then stitch other side of tape to same stripe/crease on wrong side of other quilt piece. Be sure to stitch very close to tape edges. Continue to stitch tape along both pieces until all channels are formed.

3 Turn in 2 ins. on sides and bottom edge. Turn in another 2 ins. and stitch down. Fill channels evenly, smoothing the filling right down the channels. When satisfied with quantity of filling, fold over top edge and stitch in same way as sides.

4 You can attach two 40-in. ties to the end of your quilt to attach it to your bed or to tie it into a bundle for storage for times when it's not in use.

Chair Pillows

Chair pillows are an easy way to add comfort and style to wooden chairs. Choose a washable fabric to complement your color scheme.

MATERIALS

For each pillow:
- [ ] two 20 x 18-in. pieces sturdy fabric
- [ ] synthetic stuffing

For piped pillow:
- [ ] 60 ins. corded piping (see page 42)
- [ ] 2¼ yds. of 6-in.-wide strips for ties

For walled pillow:
- [ ] 3½ yds. corded piping (see page 42)
- [ ] 20 ins. of 3-in.-wide strip for wall
- [ ] 2¼ yds. of 3-in.-wide strip for ties

For ruffled pillow:
- [ ] 5¼ yds. of 4-in.-wide ruffle
- [ ] 2¼ yds. of 3-in.-wide strip for closure strip and ties

Note: ½-in. seams allowed. Same pattern outline applies for all pillows.

Piped Pillow

METHOD

Pattern Outline:
See Pull Out Pattern Sheet at back of book.

1 Cut out two pillow pieces. Mark positions of small quilted squares. Make piping and attach to right side of pillow front as instructed in Down To Detail on page 42.

2 Cut strips into four 20-in. lengths. Fold each in half with right sides facing and stitch around one long and one short end. Turn and iron. Place ties at markings on right side of front, matching raw edges. Stitch along piping stitchline.

3 Place pillow back and front together with right sides facing. Stitch around edge following piping stitchline, leaving opening for stuffing at center back. Turn pillow to right side. Iron well.

4 Stitch around four little squares securely at markings. Stuff pillow, being sure to distribute stuffing evenly. Hand-stitch opening.

Walled Pillow

METHOD

1 Cut two pillow pieces as for Piped Pillow. Mark positions of small quilted squares. Make piping as instructed in Down To Detail on page 42.

2 Stitch piping around right side of each pillow piece.

3 Starting at a back corner, pin wall around one pillow piece over piping stitchline, matching raw edges. Determine where back seam should be in wall. Mark seamline, trim away excess fabric if necessary. Stitch seam. Stitch pinned edge of wall to pillow, following piping stitchline.

4 Make ties as for Piped Pillow. Pin ties in position onto remaining pillow piece.

With right sides facing, align remaining pillow piece on raw edge of wall, pin and stitch following piping stitchline, leaving an opening at back for stuffing. Turn and iron. Quilt four squares securely as marked. Stuff pillow evenly. Fold in wall seam allowance at opening, pin to piping stitchline. Stitch.

Ruffled Pillow

METHOD

1 Cut two pillow pieces as for Piped Pillow. Mark positions of small quilted squares.

2 Join ruffle strips where required. Fold ruffle over double with wrong sides together and raw edges matching. Gather raw edges together. With right sides facing and raw edges matching, stitch ruffle around sides and front of one piece. Place remaining piece over top, with right sides facing. Stitch around trimmed edges in ruffle stitchline. Turn and iron.

3 Cut two 16-in. pieces from tie strip. Fold over double with right sides facing. Stitch one long side and short end. Turn and iron. Stitch quilting squares securely as marked.

4 Center remaining strip across back of pillow, matching one long side to one raw edge of pillow and ruffle ends. Stitch matched edge. Stuff pillow evenly. Fold over ½ in. on raw edges of strip. Fold strip over double and pin to close back of pillow, enclose raw ends of ruffle and form ties extending on each side. Stitch around ties over all folded edges. Iron.

5 Stitch 16-in. ties firmly to extension ties where ruffle meets pillow.

Pillows

Nothing adds instant decorating impact like beautiful pillows. They are easy to make, take little fabric and come in so many shapes and styles that you'll find it difficult to decide which ones to make.

Note: ½-in. seams allowed.

Ruffled Piped Pillow

MATERIALS
- ☐ 16-in. square for front, and two backs, each 16 x 8½ ins.
- ☐ 2 yds. piping (optional)
- ☐ 12-in.-long zipper
- ☐ 3½ yds. of ruffle in desired style
- ☐ 16-in.-square pillow form

METHOD
1 Make two-color ruffle as instructed in Down To Detail on page 42.

2 With right sides facing and raw edges matching, stitch piping (if desired) and then ruffle around edge of pillow front as instructed in Down To Detail on page 42. If attaching ruffle after piping, stitch over stitchline for piping. Insert zipper in back following instructions in Down To Detail on page 42.

3 Place back and front together with right sides facing. Stitch around outside edge following stitchline of piping. Clip away bulk at corners. Turn and iron.

Striped Pillow

MATERIALS
- ☐ four matching triangles, each 23 x 17 x 17 ins. for front, and two backs, each 23 x 12½ ins.
- ☐ 23-in.-square thin synthetic batting
- ☐ 12-in.-long zipper
- ☐ 16 in.-square pillow form

METHOD
1 Carefully join two triangles along one 17-in. seam and iron seam open. Repeat for other two triangles. Carefully matching stripes, stitch two halves of pillow front together. Iron seam open.

2 Baste batting to wrong side of pillow front.

3 Insert zipper in pillow back as instructed in Down To Detail on page 42. Open zipper. Place front and back together with right sides facing and stitch

around outside edge. Trim excess bulk from corners and seams. Turn to right side and iron.

4 Carefully pin through all thicknesses 3½ ins. from edge to form flange. Stitch along pin line.

Appliqued Piped Pillow

METHOD
1 Cut applique from fabric and attach motif onto pillow front as for the easy Applique Pillow on page 88, having the stitching on the edge of the motif, rather than ½ in. away. Choose thread to harmonize with background fabric and motif.

2 Make piping and pillow in exactly the same way as the Ruffled Piped Pillow, omitting ruffle.

Piped Pillow with Contrast Band

MATERIALS
- ☐ 16-in. square for front, and two backs, each 16 x 8½ ins.
- ☐ four strips border fabric, each 13 x 4 ins.
- ☐ 2 yds. contrast piping (see page 42 for making instructions)
- ☐ 12-in.-long zipper
- ☐ 16-in.-square pillow form

METHOD
1 Trim short ends of strips to perfect diagonals. Join strips to form mitered square which fits pillow 1½ ins. from outside edge. Clip ½ in. in on corner seam. Iron seams open. Iron under ½ in. on inside and outside edges of square. Pin square onto pillow front and edgestitch into place.

2 Attach piping and insert zipper as instructed in Down To Detail on page 42. Open zipper. Place front and back together with right sides facing. Stitch around outside edge. Trim excess bulk from corners and seams. Turn and iron.

Ruffled Pillow with Contrast Band

MATERIALS
- [ ] 16-in. square for front, and two backs, each 16 x 8½ ins.
- [ ] four strips border fabric, each 16 x 4 ins.
- [ ] 3½ yds. of gathered ruffle
- [ ] 12-in.-long zipper
- [ ] 16-in.-square pillow form

METHOD

1 Trim short ends of border strips to perfect diagonals. Join strips together to form mitered square. Clip ½ in. in on corner seams. Iron seams open. Iron under ½ in. on inside edge of border.

2 Pin border to pillow front, matching outside edges. Edgestitch inside edge of border onto front. Attach ruffle as instructed in Down To Detail on page 42.

3 Insert zipper as instructed in Down To Detail on page 42. Open zipper. Place front and back together with right sides facing. Stitch around outside edge in previous stitchline. Trim excess bulk at corners and seams. Turn and iron.

Pillow with Padded Edge and Contrast Band

MATERIALS
- [ ] 22-in. square for front, and two backs, each 22 x 12 ins.
- [ ] four strips border fabric, each 16 x 4 ins.
- [ ] 22-in. square thin synthetic batting
- [ ] 12-in.-long zipper
- [ ] 16-in.-square pillow form

METHOD

1 Trim short ends of border strips to perfect diagonals. Join strips to form mitered square which fits on pillow front 3 ins. from edge. Clip ½ in. in on corner seams. Iron seams open. Iron under ½ in. on inside and outside edges of border square. Pin square onto pillow front and edgestitch into place. Baste batting to wrong side of trimmed pillow front.

2 Insert zipper as instructed in Down To Detail on page 42. Open zipper. Place pillow front and back together with right sides facing. Stitch around outside edge. Trim excess bulk from corners and seams. Turn and iron.

3 Carefully pin through all thicknesses along outside edge of border to form 3-in.-wide flange. Stitch down along previous stitchline.

Floral Pillow with Contrast Edge

MATERIALS
- [ ] 16-in. square for front, and two backs, each 16 x 8½ ins.
- [ ] eight strips for flange, each 22 x 4 ins.
- [ ] four strips thin synthetic batting, each 22 x 4 ins.
- [ ] 12-in.-long zipper
- [ ] 16-in.-square pillow form

METHOD

1 Baste batting strips to wrong side of four flange strips. Trim short ends to perfect diagonals and join strips to form mitered square. Trim excess batting from seams. Turn and iron. Join other four strips in same way, omitting batting.

2 Place two flange squares together with right sides facing and stitch around outside edge. Trim excess bulk at corners and seams. Turn and iron. Baste inside edges together.

3 With right sides facing, pin pillow front to inside edge of flange, matching raw edges and corners. Stitch through all thicknesses.

4 Insert zipper as instructed in Down To Detail on page 42. Open zipper. Place front and back together with right sides facing, tucking flange out of the way and stitching around outside edge in previous stitchline. Trim excess bulk at corners and seams. Turn to right side through zipper opening and iron.

Down to DETAIL

Pillows

To make continuous corded piping

1 Cut a piece of fabric as shown in Figure 1. Mark bias strips as shown.

2 Fold fabric with right sides together, so that points A and B are matching. Note that one strip width extends at each side. Join AA to BB with a 1/4-in. seam. Iron seam open (see Figure 2).

3 Cut along bias strip marked lines, giving you one continuous strip of bias fabric. Fold this strip in half over cable cord. Secure cord inside fabric by stitching close to cord, through all thicknesses using the zipper foot of your machine. Match sewing thread to fabric.

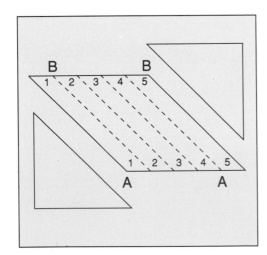

Figure 1

To attach piping

1 With right sides facing and raw edges matching, pin piping around edge of pillow front, clipping piping seam allowances at corners. Cut 3/4 in. of cord out of one end of piping to lessen bulk at overlap. Overlap piping ends.

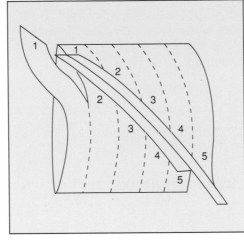

Figure 2

2 Sew on piping using the zipper foot of your machine.

To insert a zipper

1 Cut two pillow backs. With right sides facing, match two long sides of pillow backs. Stitch both ends closed in a 3/4-in. seam, leaving an opening the length of your zipper, at the center. Iron seams open.

2 Insert zipper into opening. Open zipper before joining pillow back and front in order to turn pillow through zipper opening (see picture below).

To make a one-color ruffle

1 Cut ruffle 9 ins. wide and twice the circumference of your pillow in length. For a 16-in. pillow your ruffle strip will measure 3 1/2 yds x 9 ins. If necessary, join strips to make required length. Join short ends of ruffle to form a circle.

2 Fold over double, lengthwise, with wrong sides together and raw edges matching. Gather ruffle 1/2 in. in from raw edge. Pull up gathering to fit pillow front (see picture above).

To make a two-color ruffle

1 Cut two ruffles, one 5 1/2 ins. wide and another in contrasting fabric 4 1/2 ins. wide and twice the circumference of your pillow in length.

2 With right sides facing match one long raw edge of each strip and stitch 1/2 in. from edge. Iron seam to one side. Join short ends of ruffle to make a circle.

3 Fold fabric over double, lengthwise, with wrong sides together and raw edges matching. Iron. Gather ruffle 1/2 in. in from raw edge. Draw up gathering to fit outside edge of pillow front.

4 This technique gives a ruffle with the appearance of a contrast fabric binding at the outer edge (see picture above.)

Bed Linen

Making your own bed linen is easy, lets you create your own decorating scheme and can save you money too! Remember to measure the bed carefully – small differences won't matter for flat sheets, but accuracy is important for dust ruffles.

FABRIC REQUIRED FOR SHEETS AND QUILT COVER

	Queen Size	Double Bed Size	Single Bed Size
Flat Sheet	3¹/₄ yds.	2³/₄ yds.	2 yds.
Fitted Sheet	3 yds.	2¹/₂ yds.	1³/₄ yds.
Quilt Cover	4³/₄ yds. to finish at 2¹/₂ yds. x width of sheeting	4 yds. to finish at 2 yds. x width of sheeting	3¹/₄ yds. to finish at 1¹/₂ yds. x width of sheeting

FABRIC REQUIRED FOR PILLOWCASES

Plain Pillowcase	20 ins.
Ruffled Pillowcase	28 ins.
Buttoned Pillowcase	20 ins. main fabric; 20 x 6 ins. (or width desired) contrast
Flanged Pillowcase	28 ins.

Before You Begin

❏ Sheeting width varies. The quantities given in the following instructions are calculated on standard sizes of manufactured sheets and quilt covers.

❏ All sheets and quilt covers are cut with selvages forming the top and bottom edges while sides have raw edges which will be hemmed.

❏ Quilt covers should be made to fit individual quilts. Measure your own quilt before purchasing materials. Consider using contrasting and complementary colors or prints for the front and back of your quilt.

MATERIALS
☐ ¹/₂-in.-wide elastic for fitted sheets
☐ approx 4¹/₂ yds. of ³/₄-in.-wide cotton twill tape for quilt cover
☐ 5 small buttons for buttoned pillowcase
☐ 20-in.-long zipper for quilt. If long zipper is not available, two long dress zippers, stitched with pull-tabs at center, will do very well. Snap fasteners on a fabric strip are also suitable.

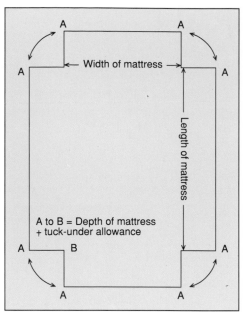

Above: Diagram for cutting and stitching a Fitted Sheet
Left: Sheets, Pillowcases and Dust Ruffle

4 You may like to stitch ties of cotton tape inside cover at each corner and on each corner of quilt. Tie these to keep quilt in place within cover.

Dust Ruffle

It is difficult to give exact measurements and fabric quantities as beds are different heights. The base is same size as mattress top plus seam allowances. Ruffle is same depth as height of bed base from floor plus hems, and length of ruffle should be twice bed length plus bed width x 2.

1 For beds with no bed posts or board at foot, simply hem bedhead end of base. Join ruffle into one continuous strip. Hem short ends and one long edge. Gather remaining raw edge. Stitch ruffle around raw edges of ruffle base.

2 For beds with bedstead posts, hem head end as above. Finish ruffle on either side of posts, with short edges hemmed and butted together at corners. Hem one long side, gather the other and attach to base as above.

3 You can stitch ties on either side at top to tie around bed posts or base legs if you wish. Stitch 4 ins. of elastic to one end of each tie and other end of elastic to ruffle corner. Elastic will take strain off ties and prevent stitching from snapping.

METHOD
Cutting and stitching methods apply to all sizes. Use ³/₄-in. seams and neaten all raw edges.

Fitted Sheets

1 Cut squares from each corner (see diagram). Join points "A". Stitch from outside edge to inner corner, forming an angle at each corner of sheet.

2 Hem around outside edge. Stitch ¹/₂-in. wide elastic to seam allowance of each corner seam, using zigzag stitch and stretching elastic as you stitch.

3 Stitch elastic around hem at corners, starting and finishing 16 ins. either side of corner seam, stretching elastic as you stitch.

Flat Sheets

1 Turn under ¹/₄ in. along raw side edges. Turn under ¹/₂ in. for hem. Iron and stitch down.

2 Turn over top and trim as desired with contrast fabric, lace, ribbon or a stenciled pattern.

Quilt Cover

1 If using sheeting, place selvages at top and bottom edges. If using cotton or polyester/cotton dress fabric, join lengths to achieve overall size.

2 If using a zipper to close quilt cover, join ends of one short side, leaving correct opening for zipper, using a ³/₄-in. seam. Iron open seam allowance. Insert zipper. Open zipper. Turn quilt cover so that right sides are facing. Stitch front to back right around, using a ³/₄-in. seam allowance. Turn quilt cover to right side through zipper opening.

3 Place front and back together with right sides facing. Stitch all around with ³/₄-in. seam allowance and leaving a 40-in. opening at one narrow end. Stitch down seam allowances at opening, then stitch on small buttons and stitch buttonholes.

Down to DETAIL

Pillowcases

Plain Pillowcase

1 Cut fabric 20 ins. x 1³/₄ yds. Turn in raw edges on both short ends. Stitch ¹/₂-in. hem on one end and 2-in. hem on other. Trim on 2-in. hem end as desired.

2 Fold fabric as shown in diagram. Stitch down sides, turn and iron.

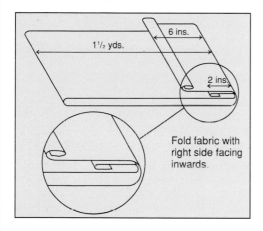

Fold fabric with right side facing inwards.

Ruffled Pillowcase

1 Cut a front piece 31 x 20 ins. Cut two backing pieces, one 28 x 20 ins. and another 9 x 20 ins. Cut piece for ruffle 5³/₄ yds. x 20 ins.

2 Join short ends of ruffle strip. Fold over double with raw edges matching. Gather raw edges.

3 Stitch ruffle around all edges of front piece, with right sides facing and raw edges matching.

4 Narrow hem one 20-in. edge of each backing piece. Place both back pieces on right side of front piece with right sides facing, overlapping hemmed edges and having outside edges matching. Stitch around outside edge through all thicknesses. Turn and iron.

Buttoned Pillowcase

1 Cut a piece 1³/₄ yds. x 20 ins. Cut another 20 x 6 ins.

2 With right side of small piece facing wrong side of larger piece, stitch together across one short end. Iron small piece to right side of larger piece.

3 Iron under ¹/₂ in. on other 20-in. raw edge of small piece. Tuck contrast piping under this pressed edge and stitch through all thicknesses. Iron under ¹/₂ in. on other 20-in. raw edge of larger piece then press under 2 ins. Stitch. Fold pillowcase with right sides together and short ends matching, securing stitching firmly at opening edge. Turn and iron.

4 Make five evenly spaced buttonholes across front 1¹/₂ ins. down from opening. Sew corresponding buttons to inside of back opening. Bind opening edges to match contrast panel if desired.

Flanged Pillowcase

1 Cut one front piece 28 x 38 ins. Cut two back pieces, one 31¹/₂ x 28 ins. and another 14 x 28 ins.

2 Narrow hem one 28-in. end of each back piece. Place back pieces on front piece with right sides facing, hemmed edges of back pieces overlapping and all raw edges matching. Stitch around outside edge. Trim corners of bulk. Turn to right side and iron.

3 Stitch all around pillowcase 3 ins. in from stitched edge to form flange. To trim, add lace or trimmings at this stitchline and insert ¹/₈-in.-wide satin ribbon through lace. Tie ends of ribbons into bows at corners.

Light
and
Shade

These drapes and shades are so simple and so effective. There's no sacrificing any of their charm. Now tie your room's color scheme together and cover your lamp shades with related fabrics. So easy. Clever you.

The dramatic impact of this decorative screen is a clever balance for the matching circular tablecloth and overcloth. (See instructions for making circular cloths on page 100)

Down to DETAIL

Decorative Screens

A screen can be a practical, inexpensive room divider or simply a focal point. As everyone's needs are different, the instructions are given as a general method. Choose your own trimmings to suit your taste and your room.

Before You Begin

❏ Join several purchased louvre doors with hinges to create a screen like ours. They may be left natural, painted to give a contemporary look, or carved, sponged and stenciled.

❏ To add fabric panels, you will need sufficient fabric to cover the length of the doors with a front and back panel and a fabric strip 32 x 9 ins. for a bow for each door. Fabric panels are attached with a glue gun.

❏ To determine the size of your screen, decide where it will be located and how tall it should be to be useful.

❏ If door tops are to be shaped, design the shape on paper and transfer it to the door. You will need a fretsaw or a jigsaw to cut out the shape and sandpaper for smoothing rough edges.

MATERIALS
- ☐ louvre doors
- ☐ hinges
- ☐ screws
- ☐ screwdriver
- ☐ jigsaw or fretsaw
- ☐ sandpaper
- ☐ your choice of paint; stencils; stencil paints and brushes; sponge
- ☐ fabrics as desired
- ☐ glue gun

METHOD

1 Join doors together with hinges following manufacturer's instructions.

The taller the doors, the more support (and therefore hinges) they require.

2 To insert fabric panels, cut away top and bottom louvres from each door with a sharp chisel. If necessary, fill any holes with a suitable wood filler.

3 To paint and sponge a screen for a light, speckled effect; first paint with a base of acrylic paint and allow to dry. Using a slightly lighter color and a natural sponge, dab paint-covered sponge over base coat of paint. Remove excess paint from sponge, by dabbing onto scrap fabric. When dry, stencil as desired, following Down To Detail instructions on page 6, or decorate screen with decoupage as instructed on pages 23 and 73.

4 To cover screen with fabric panels: Measure width and length of louvres.

5 Cut a piece of fabric twice length plus 14 ins. long by twice width. Iron under ½ in. along long sides then again 1 in. Stitch along inner folded edge. Fold fabric in half lengthwise, wrong sides facing. Gather 1 in. down from fold, stitching through all thicknesses. Draw up gathers to width of louvres. Secure gathering threads. You now have a front and back panel.

6 Draw fabric through space left by bottom louvre until gathered area sits just under next louvre. Pull panels up over front and back of door and mark position of top louvre on front and back panel. Remove fabric panel from door. Fold excess fabric to wrong side 1 in. from mark on front and back panel. Gather across front and back at this mark, through all thicknesses securing folded fabric. Cut away excess fabric from 1 in. below gathering. Draw up gathers as for lower ruffle.

7 Replace fabric on door. Join front and back panels together at gathering line using glue gun, attaching fabric to top louvre at the same time.

8 To make bows: Fold a 9 x 32-in. strip of fabric with right sides facing. Cut ends at an angle. Stitch around raw edges in ½-in. seam, leaving opening for turning. Turn and press. Tie bow. Glue bow to top of screen, in center of gathers.

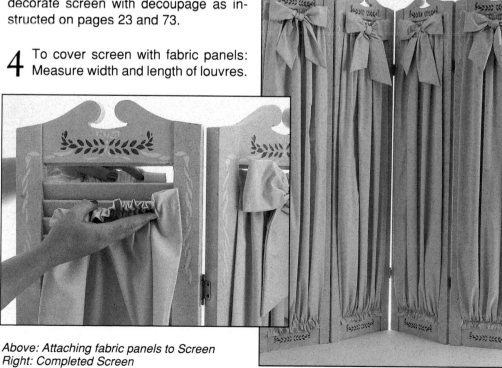

Above: Attaching fabric panels to Screen
Right: Completed Screen

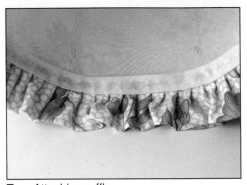

Top: Attaching ruffle
Above: Covering edge of ruffle with bias binding
Above left: Completed Lamp Shade
Below: Marking the shape of the Lamp Shade

Lamp Shade

Brighten your home with this simple recycling idea. Give your old lamp shade a new look with some of these clever suggestions for easy trims. It's more than likely that the shape of the lamp shade suits the base, so measure the existing frame to work out quantities of fabric needed.

MATERIALS

- ☐ metal lamp shade frame, stripped bare
- ☐ approximately 40 ins. of 45-in.-wide fabric for cover
- ☐ approximately 40 ins. of 45-in.-wide lining fabric
- ☐ fabric for bias binding and ruffles can be cut from scraps but if in doubt allow another 16 ins. of fabric for ruffles
- ☐ white glue
- ☐ approximately 7 yds. narrow cotton tape or leftover bias binding
- ☐ strong thread and needle
- ☐ approximately 2¼ yds. plain bias binding in lining color

METHOD

1 Wind tape or bias binding around both rings of frame until it is completely covered. Hold ends with pins until winding is complete then glue to secure.

2 Put a pin in tape at one point on shade to mark beginning and ending point. Spread lining fabric out flat and roll frame across fabric as shown. Mark position of frame as it moves across fabric leaving a 2-in. allowance on either end for seam allowances and 2 ins. each at top and bottom. Repeat for main fabric. Cut out shape as marked (see diagram below right).

3 Fit lining around frame, pinning to tape for accuracy. Pin ends closed as a seam. Remove lining from frame, sew seam as pinned. Trim seam allowance back to ½ in.

4 Place lining inside frame. Pin lining to tape with seam following line of one upright strut. Fold top and bottom edges to outside. Oversew to top and bottom rings by hand. Trim excess fabric. Repeat this process with main fabric, placing main fabric on outside and taking top and bottom edges to inside.

5 Cut sufficient 2½-in.-wide bias binding to cover top and bottom rings. Turn in ½ in. along both long sides, fold in half and glue over top and bottom rings, turning and neatly overlapping ends.

6 Cut sufficient 4-in.-wide ruffle strips to measure at least one and a half or twice total circumference of top and bottom rings, depending on thickness of your fabric. Join ends of strip to form a circle. Fold strip over double with raw edges matching. Gather raw edges. Draw up gathers to fit inside bias-trimmed top and bottom rings. Glue into place. Glue bias binding over gathered edge, tucking under short ends at overlap.

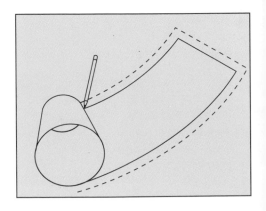

50

Gathered Drapes

So you think sewing drapes is difficult? Not these. The method can be adapted for any size rectangular window and the simple, unlined style lends itself beautifully to all sorts of trimming – stenciling, bands of ribbon trim, applique or lace edges.

METHOD

1 Iron in ½ in. on long side edges, then again 1½ ins. Stitch. Iron in ½ in. at top and bottom, then again 3 ins. Stitch. Stitch again 1½ ins. from top. This row of stitching gives you room for inserting a rod, and will create a ruffled effect.

2 Install brackets, slide drapes onto pole, adjusting gathers to fit. Hang drapes.

3 To make optional tieback: Fold strip in half lengthwise with right sides facing and raw edges matching. Stitch around all raw edges, leaving opening for turning. Turn and iron. Mark window frame or wall for hook position. Install hook and fashion tieback into a bow.

Pelmet

MATERIALS
- ☐ fabric strip twice length of track x desired depth; ruffle fabric twice length of fabric strip x 4 ins. deep
- ☐ piping length of fabric strip
- ☐ pinch pleating tape

METHOD

1 Hem short ends of pelmet and ruffle strips. Hem one long edge of ruffle and gather the other edge.

2 Stitch piping along raw edge of pelmet strip with right sides facing and raw edges even. Place ruffle over piping with right sides facing and raw edges matching. Stitch in previous stitchline.

3 Turn under 1 in. at pelmet top. Apply pleating tape following manufacturer's instructions. Draw up to fit.

Before You Begin

☐ We show you, on the Pull Out Pattern Sheet at the back of the book, how to measure your window and estimate fabric quantities. Trim quantities will depend on the size of your drape. Add stencil design and trims after sewing the drape but before you hang them.

☐ Decide whether you wish to have two drapes that open in the middle and are pulled to each side, or a single one. If two drapes are your choice, halve the width and add an extra 2 ins. to each drape for the center hem allowances. Instructions are given for one drape, simply make two using the same method.

☐ Drape tiebacks are secured by brass hooks which come in many designs.

MATERIALS
- ☐ main fabric (see illustration showing how to measure for drapes on Pull Out Pattern Sheet)
- ☐ ¾-in. diameter dowel or metal drape rod to suit your window width
- ☐ two support brackets and screws
- ☐ drape tieback hooks

Austrian Shades

These shades are the easiest of all to make, because accurate measurements are not so important. The impact depends a great deal on the fabric and its setting. Even the simplest fabrics such as voile or muslin can look very stylish made up this way.

Before You Begin

❏ Austrian shades need plenty of full-ness for a luxurious look.

❏ There are usually two main types of tape available. Both have the rings, through which you thread the draw cords, already stitched on. One type of tape has small cords on either side which draw up to gather the shade. The other type has no gathering cords. Decide whether you want a gathered or flat effect up the corded lines. Look at our photographs to help you decide. Whichever design you choose, the tape and cord quantities are the same.

❏ Placing tapes close together, say 12 ins. apart, will result in small scallops. Place them further apart for swag-like scallops. On average you will require at least three tapes, each one as long as your shade.

Fabric Shade

MATERIALS
☐ fabric piece twice width x twice length of window. If fabric needs to be joined to achieve width, use small flat seams
☐ tapes
☐ cord for each tape plus the width of shade (see illustration on page 53)
☐ if trimming edge with fabric ruffle, cut strips four times length plus twice width of shade x 9 ins.
☐ brass cleat for fastening cords
☐ knob to cover knotted ends of cords
☐ small eye-hooks – one for each tape, plus one

METHOD
Neaten any exposed raw edges. Use ¹/₂-in. seams.

1 Cut out fabric to required size and join pieces if necessary.

2 Mark tape positions. Fold fabric along these lines and press for guidelines.

3 Join ruffle strips to make required length. Fold over ½ in. at short ends, stitch. Fold ruffle strip over double, matching long raw edges and with wrong side facing. Gather raw edge. Draw up gathers and stitch ruffle to side and bottom edges of shade, with right sides facing and raw edges matching. Start and finish ruffle 3 ins. from top edge.

4 Fold in ½ in. on both side edges of shade above ruffle and stitch. Fold in ½ in. on upper edge, iron, then fold another 3 ins. Stitch. Stitch again 1 in. from previous stitching.

5 Stitch tape along guidelines, starting just above ruffles and finishing just below top casing. Make sure you have a cord ring just above ruffle on each tape.

6 Fit shade on drape pole, bunching it up to fit. Space tapes evenly.

7 Screw eye-hooks into window frame just below pole position at top of tapes and another just below one rod bracket on the side through which you will thread shade cords.

8 If using tape which draws up, draw up gathering threads on tape and secure when shade is gathered as desired. Thread draw cords through rings on each tape, starting by securing cord in bottom ring and threading it as illustrated. Thread cords through extra hook in window frame.

9 Screw cleat into window frame at a convenient height. Pass cord ends through covering knob, knot together, trim ends. Pull knob down to cover knot. Wind cord around cleat to fix height of shade.

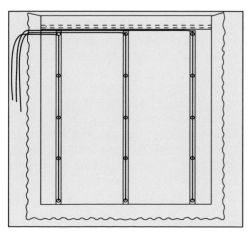

Lace Shade

The lace fabric we used has scalloped edges and as it was not wide enough for the window, two lengths were joined.

MATERIALS

☐ four times length of window in scalloped edge lace

☐ all other requirements are as for Fabric Shade

METHOD

1 Cut both scalloped edges off center panel and set aside to be used later. Cut another length down the middle and join each half either side of center panel. The scallops on the outside edges become the ruffle.

2 Trim top and bottom of shade with cut-off scallops. Cut a length of scallops to width of shade. Hem short ends. Using a ½-in. seam, sew scallops to top of shade with right side of scallops facing wrong side of shade. Press scallops to right side. Stitch across 3 ins. down from top, then again 1½ ins. from previous stitching. Gather remaining scallops along both short ends and long side. Apply whole of gathered edge to bottom of shade to give appearance of a continuation of side ruffle.

3 Make shade in same way as Fabric Shade on page 52. Fabric, tapes, cords, brackets, rod, eye-hooks, knob and cleat instructions are all identical.

Below left: Threading of cords
Below: Fabric Shade

Crochet Blind

A delicate crochet window blind not only has a practical use but adds a touch of old-world charm.

GAUGE
Size of motif = approximately 7 ins. square

MEASUREMENTS
Approximately 35½ ins. wide x 30 ins. long
The blind shown uses twenty motifs arranged in four rows of five motifs. To make a larger or smaller blind, make more or fewer motifs, or, for a small adjustment, simply block blind to size desired.

MATERIALS
☐ 300 gms crochet cotton size 20, in color of your choice. (It is advisable to purchase required number of balls in one dye lot before beginning.)
☐ steel crochet hook size 9 (1.25 mm) or size required to obtain gauge.
☐ 40 ins. of ⅛-in-wide ribbon
☐ 9 small ribbon roses
☐ 11 curtain rings
Note: Two motifs can be worked from 30 gms of thread

ABBREVIATIONS
ch = chain; sl st = slip stitch; sc = single crochet; dc = double crochet; tr = treble (triple) crochet; d tr = double treble (thread over hook three times); tr tr = triple treble (thread over hook 4 times); quad tr = quadruple treble (thread over hook 5 times); lp = loop; rep = repeat; sp(s) = space(s); st(s) = stitche(s)

METHOD
First Motif
Ch 12, sl st in first ch to form a ring.
1st rnd: Ch 3, dc in ring, (ch 3, 2 dc in ring) 7 times; ch 3, join with sl st in top of first ch-3.
2nd rnd: Sl st in next dc and in next sp, ch 3, (2 dc, ch 3, 3 dc in same sp) — starting shell made, *ch 3, dc in next sp, ch 3, (3 dc, ch 3, 3 dc in next sp) — one shell made; rep from * omitting a shell at end of last rep, join with sl st in top of first ch-3.
3rd rnd: Sl st in each of next 2 dc, ch 3, *work a shell in next sp, dc in next dc, (ch 3, dc in next sp) twice, ch 3, skip 2 dc, dc in next dc; rep from * omitting 1 dc at end of last rep, join with sl st in top of first ch-3.

4th rnd: Sl st in each of next 2 dc, ch 3, *dc in next dc, a shell in next sp, dc in each of next 2 dc, (ch 3, dc in next sp) 3 times, ch 3, skip 2 dc, dc in next dc; rep from * omitting 1 dc at end of last rep, join with sl st in top of first ch-3.
5th rnd: Sl st in each of next 2 dc, ch 3, *dc in each of next 2 dc, a shell in next sp, dc in each of next 3 dc, (ch 3, dc in next sp) 4 times, ch 3, skip 2 dc, dc in next dc; rep from * 1 omitting dc at end of last rep, join with sl st in top of first ch-3.
6th rnd: Sl st in each of next 2 dc, ch 3, *dc in each of next 3 dc, a shell in next sp, dc in each of next 4 dc, (ch 3, dc in next sp) 5 times, ch 3, skip 2 dc, dc in next dc; rep from * omitting 1 dc at end of last rep, join with sl st in top of first ch-3.
7th rnd: Sl st in each of next 2 dc, ch 3, *dc in each of next 4 dc, a shell in next sp, dc in each of next 5 dc, (ch 3, dc in next sp) 6 times, ch 3, skip 2 dc, dc in next dc; rep from * omitting 1 dc at end of last rep, join with sl st in top of first ch-3.
8th rnd: Sl st in each of next 2 dc, ch 3, *dc in each of next 5 dc, a shell in next sp, dc in each of next 6 dc, (ch 3, dc in next sp) 7 times, ch 3, skip 2 dc, dc in next dc; rep from * omitting 1 dc at end of last rep, join with sl st in top of first ch-3.
9th rnd: Sl st in each of next 2 dc, ch 3, *dc in each of next 6 dc, a shell in next sp, dc in each of next 7 dc, (ch 3, dc in next sp) 8 times, ch 3, skip 2 dc, dc in next dc; rep from * omitting 1 dc at end of last rep, join with sl st in top of first ch-3.
10th rnd: Sl st in each of next 2 dc, ch 3, * dc in each of next 8 dc, a shell in next sp, dc in each of next 9 dc, (ch 3, dc in next sp) 4 times, ch 3, skip 1 dc and 2 ch, dc in each of next 3 sts, ch 3, skip 2 ch and 1 dc (dc in next sp, ch 3) 4 times, skip 2 dc, dc in next dc; rep from * omitting 1 dc at end of last rep, join with sl st in top of first ch-3.
11th rnd: Sl st in each of next 2 dc, ch 3, *dc in each of next 9 dc, a shell in next sp, dc in each of next 10 dc, (ch 3, dc in next sp) 4 times, ch 3, skip 1 dc and 2 ch, dc in each of next 5 sts, ch 3, skip 2 ch and 1 dc, (dc in next sp, ch 3) 4 times, skip 2 dc, dc in next dc; rep from * omitting 1 dc at end of last rep, join with sl st in top of first ch-3.

12th rnd: Sl st in each of next 2 dc, ch 3, *dc in each of next 10 dc, a shell in next sp, dc in each of next 11 dc, (ch 3, dc in next sp) 4 times, ch 3, skip 1 dc and 2 ch, dc in each of next 7 sts, ch 3, skip 2 ch and 1 dc, (dc in next sp, ch 3) 4 times, skip 2 dc, dc in next dc; rep from * omitting 1 dc at end of last rep, join with sl st in top of first ch-3.
13th rnd: Sl st in each of next 2 dc, ch 3, *dc in each of next 11 dc, a shell in next sp, dc in each of next 12 dc (ch 3, dc in next sp) 4 times, ch 3, skip 1 dc and 2 ch, dc in each of next 9 sts, ch 3, skip 2 ch and 1 dc, (dc in next sp, ch 3) 4 times, skip 2 dc, dc in next dc; rep from * omitting 1 dc at end of last rep, join with sl st in top of first ch-3.
14th rnd: Sl st in each of next 2 dc, ch 3, *dc in each of next 12 dc, a shell in next sp, dc in each of next 13 dc, (ch 3, dc in next sp) 4 times, ch 3, skip 1 dc and 2 ch, dc in each of next 11 sts, ch 3, skip 2 ch and 1 dc, (dc in next sp, ch 3) 4 times, skip 2 dc, dc in next dc; rep from * omitting 1 dc at end of last rep, join with sl st in top of first ch-3.
15th rnd: Sl st in each of next 2 dc, ch 3, *dc in each of next 13 dc, a shell in next sp, dc in each of next 14 dc, (ch 3, dc in next sp) 4 times, ch 3, skip 1 dc and 2 ch, dc in each of next 13 sts, ch 3, skip 2 ch and 1 dc, (dc in next sp, ch 3) 4 times, skip 2 dc, dc in next dc; rep from * omitting 1 dc at end of last rep, join with sl st in top of first ch-3.
16th rnd: Sl st in each of next 2 dc, ch 3, *dc in each of next 14 dc, a shell in next sp, dc in each of next 15 dc, (ch 3, dc in next sp) 4 times, ch 3, skip 1 dc and 2 ch, dc in each of next 15 sts, ch 3, skip 2 ch and 1 dc, (dc in next sp, ch 3) 4 times, skip 2 dc, dc in next dc; rep from * omitting 1 dc at end of last rep, join with sl st in top of first ch-3.
17th rnd: Sl st in each of next 2 dc, ch 3, *dc in each of next 15 dc, a shell in next sp, dc in each of next 16 dc, (ch 3, dc in next sp) 4 times, ch 3, skip 1 dc and 2 ch, dc in each of next 17 sts, ch 3, skip 2 ch and 1 dc (dc in next sp, ch 3) 4 times, skip 2 dc, dc in next dc; rep from * omitting 1 dc at end of last rep, join with sl st in top of first ch-3.
18th rnd: Sc in same place as sl st, *(ch 1, skip 1 dc, sc in next dc) 9 times, ch 1, (sc, ch 3 and sc in next sp), ch 1, sc in next dc, (ch 1, skip dc, 2 sc in next dc) 9 times, (ch 1, sc in next sp, ch 1, sc in next dc) 5 times, (ch 1, skip 1 dc, sc in next dc) 8 times, (ch 1, sc in next sp, ch 1, sc in next dc) 5 times; rep from * omitting 1 sc at end of last rep, join with a sl st in first sc. End off.

Second motif

Work as for first motif for 18 rnds.

19th rnd: Sc in same place as sl st, (ch 1, skip 1 dc, sc in next dc) 9 times, ch 1, sc in next sp, ch 1, sc in corresponding lp on first motif, ch 1, sc in same sp on second motif, sc in next ch-1 sp on first motif, sc in next dc on second motif, (sc in next ch-1 sp on first motif, skip 1 dc on second motif, sc in next dc) 9 times, (sc in next ch-1 sp on first motif, sc in next sp on second motif, sc in next ch-1 sp on first motif, sc in next dc on second motif) 5 times, (sc in next ch-1 sp on first motif, skip 1 dc on second motif, sc in next dc) 8 times, (sc in next ch-1 sp on first motif, sc in next sp on second motif, sc in next ch-1 sp on first motif, sc in next dc on second motif) 5 times, (sc in next ch-1 sp on first motif, skip 1 dc on second motif, sc in next dc) 9 times, sc in next ch-1 sp on first motif, sc in next sp on second motif, ch 1, sc in next lp on first motif, ch 1, sc in same sp on second motif and complete as first motif.

Make five rows of four motifs, joining each as second motif was joined to first motif. Where four corners meet, join third and fourth motifs to joining of previous motifs.

Lower Edging

1st row: With work right-side up, attach thread to first free ch-3 lp at lower edge. Ch 3, *(dc in next sc, dc in next ch-1 sp) 9 times, dc in next sc, ch 17, skip eleven ch-1 sps, 1 d tr in next sp, ch 4, skip 1 sp, tr tr in next sp, (ch 4, 1 quad tr in next sp) twice, ch 4, tr tr in next sp, ch 4, skip next sp, 1 d tr in next sp, ch 17, skip eleven ch-1 sps, (dc in next sc, dc in next sp) 10 times, dc over sc joining motifs, dc in next sp; rep from * along lower edge, omitting 2 dc at end of last rep and working last dc in last free ch-3 lp, ch 3, TURN.

2nd row: Skip first dc, dc in each of next 17 dc, *18 dc in next lp, dc in next d tr, 5 dc in next lp, dc in next tr tr, (5 dc in next lp, dc in next quad tr) twice, 5 dc in next lp, dc in next tr tr, 5 dc in next lp, dc in next d tr, 18 dc in next lp, skip 2 dc, dc in each of next 37 dc; rep from * omitting 19 dc at end of last rep and working last dc in top of last ch-3, ch 3, TURN.

3rd row: Skip first dc, dc in each of next 15 dc, *skip 2 dc, dc in each of next 67 dc, skip 2 dc, dc in each of next 33 dc; rep from * omitting 17 dc at end of last rep and working last dc in top of last ch-3, ch 3, TURN.

4th row: Skip first dc, dc in next dc, (ch 3, skip 3 dc, dc in next dc) 3 times, *(skip 2 dc, dc in next dc, ch 3) 22 times, dc in next dc, skip 2 dc, dc in next dc, **(ch 3, skip 3 dc, dc in next dc) 7 times; rep from * ending last rep at **, (ch 3, skip 3 dc, dc in next dc) 3 times, dc in top of last ch-3. End off.

Top edging

1st row: With work right-side up, attach thread to first free ch-3 lp at top edge. Ch 4, *dc in next sp, ch 1; rep from * along top edge ending with dc in top of last ch-3 lp. End off.

To complete

Dampen work and block to measurements, then let dry completely. Thread ribbon through spaces of top edging, then sew curtain rings at each edge and evenly spaced between. Decorate lower edge with ribbon roses as shown in photo or as desired.

For the Children

There are always special things to make for your growing family. This soft activity doll is perfect for little fingers to explore, the doll's house will delight a growing child, and you will remember those all-too-short childhood years with a clever collage of family photographs.

Doll's House

Providing hours of fun, this doll's house is made from cardboard cartons covered with homespun or recycled fabric. You will find that most materials needed are already in your work box or scrap drawer.

MATERIALS

- [ ] one carton in good condition for each level of the house
- [ ] white glue
- [ ] spray-adhesive or a glue gun
- [ ] masking tape
- [ ] assorted scraps of lace, wallpaper, fabric, plain fabric for exterior walls; paper towel roll for chimney; firm, plain cardboard for stairs
- [ ] floral cut-edge ribbon or decorative craft ribbon
- [ ] paper cups for table and chairs; empty matchboxes for chest of drawers; notice-board pins for drawer handles; scrap of silver paper for wall mirror; assorted ribbon lengths; small square box for bed; four bamboo skewers for bedposts; scraps of synthetic batting or cotton wool; cardboard or another carton to cut up for roof
- [ ] sharp craft knife
- [ ] clothespin peg for doll; pipe cleaners
- [ ] scraps of fabric, lace and wool for doll

METHOD

Instructions are given for a two-level house. Eliminate stairs if you wish to make a single-level house.

1 Glue two cartons securely together on top of one another and upside down, so that bottom of lower carton forms floor of upper level.

2 Cut out front of each carton, leaving approximately 4 in. border at sides and top. Cut small opening in one corner of upper floor for stairs. Cut out windows in sides and back, having first decided where you wish to place furniture.

3 Cover entire exterior of house with fabric. This is time consuming, but it is worth taking some trouble to be accurate. Cut out window areas, leaving 1 in. of fabric to fold inwards around window edges. If necessary, cover joins in fabric with craft ribbon.

4 Measure for roof, making it slightly longer than house. We used a large piece of cardboard, folded to 90 degrees, open at the ends and with a flat piece of cardboard glued inside to support the angle of the roof and form a base. You may find it easier to secure this piece with masking tape. Cut hole for chimney, remembering that it will be an oval not a circle. Glue chimney into place.

Make some simple furniture from recycled materials

5 Glue fabric carefully over internal walls, using spray-adhesive and securing fabric at corners with white glue.

6 Cut piece for staircase out of cardboard, making sure that it is long enough to reach from upper level to the floor of the lower one. Crease into steps and cover with fabric, folding edges of

Doll's House staircase

fabric to wrong side. Mark depth of steps then crease cardboard sharply along markings. Cut another piece of cardboard to form side of steps which appears to be an internal wall that extends up to form stair rail. This can be tricky. We used a glue gun because it dries so quickly. Place stairs against outside wall, pin in place. Pin internal wall against steps. Glue steps firmly into place.

7 Gather scraps of lace for drapes and glue to windows. Tie drapes back with narrow ribbons. Glue ribbon around meeting point of floor and walls to form skirting boards and around upper walls to form cornice.

8 To make bed: Fill small square box with synthetic batting or cotton wool, tuck fabric over to cover. Glue to secure. Make a small pillow from same fabric, stuff with batting or cotton wool. Cut skewers to suitable height and glue into corners of base. Place box top or square of cardboard over skewers to form canopy. Trim canopy with lace, tie bows to corners. Cover edge of bed with gathered lace or fabric to form ruffle.

9 Group eight matchboxes together to form chest of drawers. Cover with fabric to secure. Decorate chest with lace or ribbons. Push notice-board pins through "drawer" fronts to form handles, and cover

sharp points inside with a glue gun. Cut silver paper into rectangle, cut off corners and glue to wall above chest.

Chairs are circles of fabric tied to cover cut-off bottoms of plastic cups. Place a little batting or cotton wool on cup bottom, cut out circle of fabric to fit over top of upturned cup and down to floor. Tie ribbon around "chair" just below batting. Glue to secure. Tables are made in same way using a clean, upturned food can. Trim chairs and tables with lace if desired.

Clothespin Doll

Our doll has no arms but it is easy to use pipe cleaners for arms if you wish. First paint shoes, stockings and face on peg. We wrapped the doll's torso with lace to form bodice and simply gathered a length of lace and fabric for her skirt. Tie a length of ribbon around waist to secure skirt and bodice. Glue on loops of wool for hair. The cap is gathered lace, glued around head from ear to ear.

Add another shawl by trimming a triangle of pretty fabric with lace and securing it over doll's shoulders and at the center front. Glue if necessary.

A pretty Clothespin Doll that's easy to make from a clothespin and scraps of fabric, lace and ribbon

Activity Doll

This activity doll is not just a pyjama bag and pillow, but provides opportunities to practise braiding, tying shoelaces, doing up buttons and opening and closing Velcro® dots. There is even a special little handbag to fill with treasures.

MATERIALS

- ☐ one 16-in.-square pillow fabric for front, and two backs, each 16 x 8¹/₂ ins.
- ☐ 3¹/₂ yds. of 8-in.-wide ruffle fabric
- ☐ craft glue
- ☐ 12-in.-long zipper
- ☐ wool for hair
- ☐ approximately 20 ins. of 45-in.-wide quilted cream-colored fabric for body pieces
- ☐ approximately 40 ins. of 4-in.-wide broderie lace for petticoat or a larger piece of broderie fabric
- ☐ 16 ins. coordinating fabric for pinafore
- ☐ 2¹/₄ yds. of ³/₄-in.-wide braid for

- pinafore trim
- ☐ 40 ins. gingham ribbon for hair bows
- ☐ four buttons
- ☐ small quantity of Velcro tape or five sets of Velcro stick-on dots
- ☐ 6 x 6 ins. scrap plain fabric for shoes
- ☐ 28 ins. narrow ribbon or a pair of shoe laces
- ☐ 10 x 5 ins. scrap of fabric and one button for handbag
- ☐ paints for facial features
- ☐ lace doily or trimmed handkerchief for pocket
- ☐ synthetic stuffing for arms and legs
- ☐ 16-in.-square pillow form

METHOD
Pattern Outline:
See Pull Out Pattern Sheet at back of book. Use ¹/₂-in. seams and neaten any exposed raw edges.

To make body and pillow

1 Cut one body piece, one head piece, four arm pieces and four leg pieces; eight shoe fronts and two shoe backs.

2 Join ends of ruffle to form a circle. Fold over double with raw edges matching. Gather along raw edges, drawing up gathering to fit around pillow front. With raw edges matching, stitch ruffle to right side of pillow front. The pillow back pieces are joined after the doll is complete.

3 Place two shoe front pieces together with right sides facing, four times. Stitch across top and down center front. Turn and iron. Make small buttonhole at top inner corner. Place a pair of complete shoe fronts onto the bottom of front legs. Fold ¹/₂ in. on straight top edge of back

shoe pieces to inside. Pin to back leg pieces. With right sides facing, join leg pieces and arm pieces, leaving ends open. Turn. Stuff lightly.

4 Stitch head and body onto pillow front, tucking arms and legs in position underneath body piece. Stitch with zigzag or satin stitch. Tie lengths of ribbon or shoelaces into buttonholes.

To make hair

1 Wind wool around top of a chair until a thickish band is achieved. Slip it off, holding it together securely. Place scrap of ribbon about 3 ins. long underneath strands, to run at right angles to wool. Stitch through wool and ribbon to secure. Cut through loops of wool opposite ribbon.

2 Make a smaller band for bangs in same way by winding wool around a piece of cardboard about 3 1/2 ins. long. Stitch ribbon to wool in same way. Cut through opposite ribbon. Flip wool to one side, forming bangs. Stitch bangs into place across top of forehead. Center main hair piece on doll's head and stitch in place.

3 Bring wool down to ear level on either side of head, placing some glue under-

neath to secure. Gather hair into two bunches. Divide wool into three sections. Braid each section and secure by tying length of wool around end of braid. Trim uneven ends. Tie bows.

To make pinafore

1 Cut out one bodice from body shape as directed on pattern. Cut a 4-in. square for pocket. Turn in 1/4 in. on sides and lower edge. Stitch 1/2-in. hem at top. Cut an 18 x 14-in. rectangle for skirt. Round off lower corners. Gather upper edge of skirt and stitch to lower edge of bodice, matching raw edges.

2 Stitch pocket to skirt, tucking trim under edge as you sew. Trim bodice and skirt edges.

3 Make four buttonholes in bodice top. Sew buttons securely to body, giving them a shank (stem of thread wrapped around with extra thread for strength).

To make petticoat

1 Join together sufficient strips of broderie lace to create an 8 x 14-in. rectangle for skirt and a bodice of 4 x 6 ins. If using broderie fabric, cut petticoat to same size as pinafore.

2 Gather skirt across 14-in. edge. Stitch to 6-in. edge of bodice. Trim outside edge of petticoat with lace where desired.

3 Attach four Velcro dots to inside bodice, avoiding button positions on pinafore bodice. Attach corresponding Velcro dots to doll's body.

To make handbag

1 Cut an 8 x 3-in. rectangle and a strap piece 1 1/2 x 10 ins. Fold strap double lengthwise. Press in raw edges. Topstitch and edgestitch to secure.

2 Fold over 1/2 in. on one short end of bag and stitch. Cut other short end to a point. With right sides facing, fold up 2 1/2 ins. on hemmed end and stitch side seams. Fold pointed end edges to wrong side and hem. Turn to right side, iron. Make buttonhole. Sew on corresponding button. Attach handle to back of bag.

To complete

1 Experiment on paper first, then decorate doll's face using fabric pencils or paints. Use a little blusher on cheeks.

2 Finish pillow as Ruffled Piped Pillow on page 40, omitting the piping.

Pillow Quilt

MATERIALS

☐ work out how many squares of chosen size you will need. The quilt shown measures 8 squares x 6 squares, using 8-in. squares, and each pillow has a front and back so you will need about 4 1/2 yds. of 45-in.-wide fabric
☐ synthetic stuffing
☐ lengths of self-fabric rouleaux or contrasting ribbon

METHOD

Use 1/2-in. seam allowances. As finished quilt will be washable, pre-shrink all fabric before stitching.

1 Cut out required number of squares for your quilt. Place squares in pairs with right sides facing. Stitch around three sides leaving remaining side open for stuffing. Clip corners and turn pillow, making sure to push corners out accurately. Iron, turning under 1/2 in. on open edges.

2 Place pillows in rows as determined by your quilt size, butting edges together accurately. Using a zigzag or similar stitch, stitch over butted edges.

3 Stuff squares to make pillows. Take care not to place too much stuffing in each square, as it will be difficult to hold open edges together while stitching. Place

open edge of one row butted to stitched edge of next row. Stitch, using zigzag stitch or similar. Continue joining rows until desired quilt size is reached.

4 Knot ends of 10-in. lengths of rouleaux or ribbon and stitch center of lengths securely to pillow meeting points. Tie rouleaux into bows.

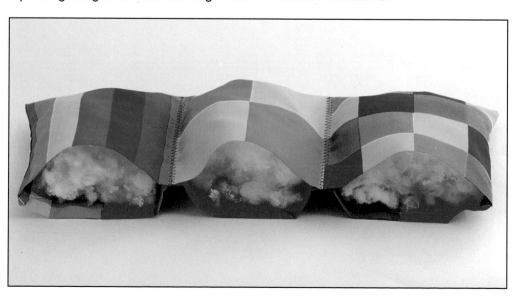

Comic Book Teddy

Don't throw away the children's comic books! Store them for a rainy day and the whole family can have fun making these terrific teddy bears.

MATERIALS

- ☐ two round balloons
- ☐ white glue
- ☐ scraps of cardboard
- ☐ four cardboard toilet roll cylinders
- ☐ transparent tape
- ☐ paper craft ribbon

METHOD

1 Mix equal parts glue and water (to make about half a cup) in a bowl to form a milky liquid.

2 Tear comic books into strips no more than 1 in. wide – narrower strips are easier to use. Place strips into glue.

Above: Joining balloons and cardboard rolls

3 Blow up two balloons for head and body. Tape over mouths of balloons. Tape them together. Cut end of each cardboard roll at an angle to allow them to fit snugly against balloons at a good angle. Tape them into position for arms and legs, checking to see that Teddy will sit well.

4 Cut two cardboard ears. Tape them into place.

5 Cover balloons with randomly glued strips. Several layers will be needed. Glue on cut-outs of colored paper for eyes, feet and nose. Glue on paper waistcoat. Tie bow tie as shown, using strips of craft ribbon. Allow Teddy to dry completely then paint with one or two coats of undiluted white glue to give a shiny, hard surface. White glue is white on application, but dries crystal clear.

Magic Quilt

These magic quilts fold up and tuck into a sewn-on pocket, making a pillow! Every sofa needs pillows and something warm to snuggle into — how convenient to unwrap the pillow and find a cuddly rug inside! Make another one for the family car.

Top: Folding Quilt
Above left: Open Quilt
Above: Quilt folded as a pillow
Cat is made following instructions on page 8

Before You Begin

❏ Make your magic quilt from pre-printed pillow panels, joined to make the correct size, or a pre-printed quilt panel with extra fabric for the pillow section. You can, of course, make a quilt from plain fabric.

❏ Remember to allow enough fabric for two sides of quilt, plus two sides of pillow piece. The average large quilt measures approximately $1^3/_4$ x $1^1/_2$ yds., with a pocket 18 ins. square.

❏ Folding the quilt may sound complicated but it's really very simple if you follow all the steps. This process can work for any size quilt, just remember to have the pillow big enough for the quilt.

MATERIALS
☐ sufficient fabric
☐ synthetic batting to fit quilt and pillow

METHOD
Use $^1/_2$-in. seams throughout.

1 Join pillow panels, if necessary, to create quilt front and back.

2 Baste batting to wrong side of quilt front. Place back and front together with right sides facing. Stitch around outside edge, leaving an opening for turning.

Turn and iron. Hand stitch opening. Topstitch edge of quilt if desired.

3 Make pillow piece using same method as for quilt. Attach to back of quilt at center of one short end by stitching around two sides and base where edges match, leaving top open. Note: If using different fabrics on front and back of quilt, be sure to make pillow in same way.

4 To fold quilt: Place quilt with front fabric facing you. Fold in one-third of quilt at each side on top of the center third. Pull pillow from back of the quilt over to front so that it encloses bottom section of folded quilt and exposes front fabric of pillow piece. Smooth out corners of pillow piece. Go to top of quilt and proceed to turn down folded quilt in sections of size of pillow piece, until last section folds neatly into pillow piece.

Picture Gallery

What to do with those drawers full of memories? Make a visual history of your child's life with a collage of cut-out photographs. When your collage is finished, frame and hang it on "permanent exhibition".

Before You Begin

❏ Collect all the old photographs cluttering the drawers. If you are doing a collage about just one person, cut that person from the photographs and arrange on the board at random, or you can start from one corner, with the earliest photos, and work to the opposite corner – perhaps taking a child from babyhood to present day.

❏ Leave enough background on some photographs to give a clue as to locations.

❏ Use sharp scissors for cutting out.

❏ Take your time arranging the photographs – lay them all out before gluing. Spray-on photography glue won't wrinkle the photographs.

Top and Right: Two Picture Galleries
Above right: Cutting out photographs

MATERIALS

❏ lots and lots of photographs
❏ photographic glue, spray-on type is excellent
❏ sharp scissors
❏ large sheet of foam board, of the kind lined both sides with cardboard

METHOD

1 Cut out pictures as shown above. Plan your layout.

2 Glue pictures in place. Do not worry if only part of a picture is glued down, the glass will hold the rest in place.

Playmat Toy Box

A recycled carton can provide hours of fun. When folded, this brightly coloured box provides handy stash-away storage for some of life's essentials such as cars, farm animals, trains and boats. Opened out it's a racetrack, a farm or your own neighbourhood.

Before You Begin

❑ Quantities of various materials will depend on the size of your box. Open out your box so that it lies flat. You will need sufficient fabric to cover the outside of your box when it is laid out flat, and brown paper to cover the inside.

❑ Measure the length of electrical tape you will need by measuring around all the edges of the box.

❑ When painting your map, add special features that make it very personal to your family. Accuracy is not as important as bright colors and interesting features.

MATERIALS
☐ firm cardboard box
☐ sharp craft knife
☐ acrylic paints
☐ paintbrushes
☐ spray-adhesive or white glue
☐ fabric and brown paper to cover (see above) and four strips fabric approximately 1¼ yds. x 9 ins. for ties
☐ approximately 7 yds. colored adhesive electrical tape
☐ thick felt-tip pen
☐ clear spray varnish

METHOD

1 Split box at corners from top to bottom. At this point, measure the box to calculate amount of fabric, brown paper and electrical tape required.

2 Glue brown paper to inside of box to provide a base for painting.

3 Using ours as a guide, mark out and paint your own road map. It may be easier to draw fences with thick felt-tip pen. Outline all features with felt-tip pen when paint is dry. Spray map with clear spray varnish.

4 Cover outside of box with fabric using glue of your choice, cutting fabric to edges of box. Cover edges with electrical tape, folding tape over edge from outside to inside.

5 With right sides facing and long raw edges matching, stitch around ties, leaving opening for turning. Clip corners, turn and iron. Place center of each tie in center of each side and 6 ins. down from box top. Glue center of tie into place as shown, leaving ends free to tie into bows, securing box sides.

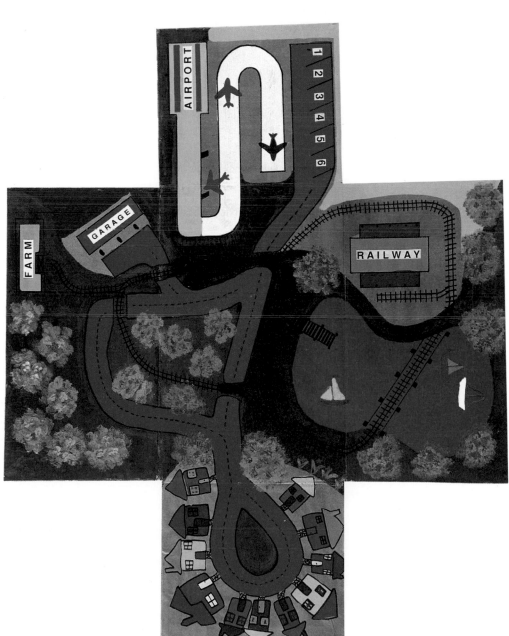

Sensational Storage

*Y*ou can add decorative touches to functional storage easily using fabric and paint. Some simple recycling will produce a padded blanket box from an old, much loved toy box, or you can try new ways with fabric decoupage to transform basic wooden boxes into instant heirlooms.

Blanket Box

This padded, chintz-covered box started life as a toy box but had become rather battered. Provided your old box is solid and has suitable timber for holding the fabric, looks don't matter!

Blanket Box before renovation

Before You Begin

❏ Decide on your fabric. Stripes are attractive, but you will have to match carefully through from front to back and over the lid. The easiest fabric to choose is one with a small print or an all-over pattern that does not require matching.

❏ Measure your own box carefully. You may find it easier to measure each panel of the box and draw these outlines and measurements on paper, then calculate fabric quantities, adding in extra for turning under and overlapping.

MATERIALS
- [ ] fabric – for our box we needed 5 yds. of outer fabric and 4½ yds. of lining
- [ ] same quantity of medium thickness synthetic batting as total fabric
- [ ] narrow, ornate furnishing braid for inner trim – we needed 5 yds. for our box
- [ ] approximately 1¾ yds. strong cord or fine chain
- [ ] four eye-hooks
- [ ] staple gun
- [ ] craft glue
- [ ] decorative upholstery tacks
- [ ] decorative handles
- [ ] three hairline hinges (these are less visible than conventional hinges)
- [ ] strong dressmakers' pins
- [ ] small tack hammer

METHOD

1 Cover box completely with batting, using a staple gun to secure edges. Cover top of box with extra batting if padding is necessary. Make sure edges are neat and that you use enough staples to keep batting edges flat.

2 First line box with lining fabric, covering panels with pieces cut to size plus a turn-under allowance. Glue these carefully into place. Take lining all the way up to lip of box.

3 Cover outside of box with cut-to-size (plus turn-under allowance) pieces of fabric, having sufficient fabric to come over top of box down into inside to overlap lining and down onto outside base. Hold fabric in place with dressmakers' pins, until you have secured side edges with decorative tacks. Space these tacks at about 1-in. intervals. When you have folded outside fabric to the inside, secure edge around box with staples, in an even line about 1½ ins. down from lip. Fold fabric neatly into corners. If necessary, sew edges together by hand to hold pieces together. Glue braid to cover line where fabrics meet, securing corners with tacks.

4 Tack outside fabric onto base, folding corners where necessary. Cover base with lining fabric and braid if desired.

5 Cover outside of lid, bringing fabric inside as for the box. Cover inside of lid with a panel of lining fabric and cover meeting line with braid. Tack corners.

6 Screw hinges to box and lid, securing lid evenly in place. Establish a suitable angle at which lid remains open, measure and fasten cords or chains to hold it at this point. Screw eye-hooks inside lid and sides of box. Tie and glue cords neatly, perhaps binding over raw edges of cord with a band of thread. Chains need to be opened with pliers and reclamped around eye-hooks.

7 Attach decorative handles to sides and center front of box.

8 Any overlap of fabric inside box that does not sit well can also be tacked.

Left: Close-up of Blanket Box showing use of braid on the inside and hairline hinges
Right: Completed Blanket Box, covered in fabric to match bedroom decor

Chest of Drawers

Take an old timber chest of drawers, add some paint and a stencil or two, some smart new handles and you will have a decorative treasure that you'll be proud to have in your home.

MATERIALS
- ☐ chest of drawers
- ☐ acrylic paints for initial coat and for stenciling pattern
- ☐ fine sandpaper
- ☐ firm plastic or Mylar® sheets for cutting stencil
- ☐ sharp craft knife
- ☐ stencil brushes
- ☐ indelible felt-tip pen for tracing stencil
- ☐ clear varnish

METHOD
See stencil design on Pull Out Pattern Sheet at back of book.

1 Remove handles. Fill any dents and marks with filler where necessary. Sand chest and apply base coat as per manufacturer's instructions. Sand again and apply second coat of paint.

2 Cut out stencil with sharp knife and apply to chest as instructed in Down To Detail on page 6. You can purchase a suitable stencil if you would rather not make your own. Apply bands of color in moldings if desired.

3 Apply sealing coat of clear varnish. Paint handles and re-attach, or fit new handles to complement the new look.

Right: Stenciling detail
Top: Chest before stenciling
Far right: Decorated Chest

Down to DETAIL

Baskets

Decorated baskets bring a warm, country look to your home. Any size basket, as long as it is solid and firmly woven, can look beautiful and still serve some practical purpose.

Basket with Stiffened Fabric Trim

Before You Begin

❏ Decide on the arrangement of your trims and, if necessary, paint your basket in colors to match. You can follow our ideas or do your own thing.

❏ Estimate fabric lengths needed for stiffened bows by tying the tape measure into a bow and placing it on the basket, adjusting the length to find the correct size.

MATERIALS
- ❏ basket
- ❏ fabric stiffener (available from craft shops)
- ❏ scissors
- ❏ trims such as fabric; lace; fabric borders used as lining or stitched into ties for bows; lengths of ribbon; artificial or handmade ribbon flowers
- ❏ white glue or glue gun
- ❏ paints and paintbrushes
- ❏ tape measure

METHOD

1 Using fingers, thoroughly cover flowers, ribbon or fabric with fabric stiffener, rubbing it well into fabric. While still wet, arrange trim on basket – either by draping, tying or pinning into place. Fabric stiffener can work as a glue, but heavier trims should be attached with extra glue when trim is dry and stiffened.

2 For a stiffened lace trim, glue smooth lace to line basket, using stiffener as glue. Trim edge with wet, stiffened, pregathered lace, adjusting gathers as it starts to dry. When completely dry and stiff, paint basket and trim as desired.

This basket has everything! We have trimmed a painted basket with a large, stiffened fabric bow and roses

Baskets with Fabric Decoupage

MATERIALS
- ❏ fabrics which feature clear motifs suitable for cutting out, preferably cotton
- ❏ sharp scissors
- ❏ white glue
- ❏ paint in colors to match fabric
- ❏ paintbrushes

METHOD

1 Paint basket and allow to dry. Cut out motifs precisely, adding elements such as leaves or extra buds to build it up. Using a paintbrush, coat motif position on basket and back of motif with glue. Place motif onto glued area, overlapping any extra pieces needed. Coat motif with more glue. Allow to dry.

2 White glue dries shiny and clear so you can continue coating entire basket with glue to seal it and give it lustre. Baskets coated in this way can be wiped with a damp cloth but not immersed in water. Clear gloss paint can be used as a sealer to give a shinier finish, but it cannot be immersed in water either.

Fabric motifs and a large bow have transformed this old basket

Baskets with Fabric Lining

MATERIALS
- ☐ square or rectangular basket
- ☐ paint in colors to complement fabric trim
- ☐ fabric strip for side panel equal to inside depth plus 2¹/₂ ins. x twice inside basket circumference
- ☐ fabric strip 7 ins. wide x same length as side panel
- ☐ fabric piece and synthetic batting same size as inside base
- ☐ white glue or clear spray varnish
- ☐ motifs from lining fabric for decoupage

METHOD

1 Paint basket if desired. Allow to dry. Decoupage outside of basket with

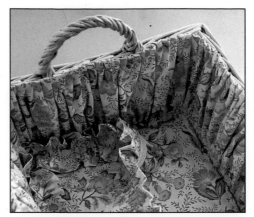

Open baskets are easy to line and decorate with decoupage

cut-out motifs and seal with clear varnish or white glue.

2 When basket is dry, line with fabric as follows: Fold over ³/₄ in. on one short end of fabric strip; iron. Fold over 2 ins. on one long edge; iron. We pleated our strip at both edges with a pleating attachment, available for all types of standard sewing machines. If this is not available, stitch a gathering stitch ¹/₂ in. from bottom raw edge and another row ³/₄ in. from top folded edge. Draw up gathers to fit inside basket, allowing folded short end to overlap raw short end at a corner. Glue panel into place, keeping folded edge at rim of basket and lower gathering at bottom.

3 Stitch fabric for bottom and batting together close to edge, glue into basket, covering edge of side panel.

Cut out motifs from lining fabric to use for decoupage

4 Fold 2 ins. on long edges of 7-in.-wide strip inwards so that edges overlap at centre. Fold in ³/₄ in. on one short end. Iron. Stitch two parallel gathering rows along overlap. Draw up gathers to fit bottom

circumference of basket. Starting at one corner, glue gathered area of strip around bottom, covering fabric meeting line. Overlap folded end over raw end and glue into place.

Litter Basket

MATERIALS
- ☐ round litter basket
- ☐ fabric strip which is height of basket side plus 12 ins. x one and a half times circumference of basket lip
- ☐ two lengths ¹/₂-in.-wide ribbon or cord, each twice circumference of basket – (this is not seen so may be any color)

These pretty covers are easy to remove for laundering

METHOD

1 With right sides facing, stitch short sides of fabric strip together in ¹/₂-in. seam. Neaten raw edges.

2 Fold over ¹/₂ in. on one raw edge, then again ³/₄ in. Stitch, leaving opening at seam for inserting cord or ribbon. Fold ¹/₂ in. inwards on remaining raw edge; iron. Fold another 3¹/₂ ins. Stitch along first fold. Iron 3¹/₂-in.-wide edge back onto right side, folding at stitching. Stitch again through all thicknesses ³/₄ in. away, forming a 2³/₄-in. ruffle when gathered.

3 On inside, unpick seam between stitching rows to allow for cord insertion. Insert one cord length each into top and bottom casings. Pull fabric over basket and draw up cord around bottom. Draw up top cord, adjusting gathers to fit. Tie cords into bows and tuck out of sight.

Hat Boxes

Decorated hat boxes have made a welcome return. They are great for storing all sorts of things – including tiny hats!

Left: *Fabric Covered Box; Decoupage Box*
Above: *Inside of Decoupage Box*

Before You Begin

❑ How much fabric and batting you need will depend on the size of your box, whether you are covering it or just lining it. We used approximately 1½ yds. each of 45-in.-wide fabric and batting for the Fabric Covered Box.

❑ Allow ³/₄-in. turn-under and overlap allowances around edges of all fabric and batting, unless instructed otherwise.

MATERIALS
- ☐ sturdy, lidded wooden box
- ☐ two pieces firm cardboard for bottom and lid lining
- ☐ white glue
- ☐ small paintbrush to apply glue

For Fabric-covered Box:
- ☐ fabric to cover
- ☐ medium thickness synthetic batting
- ☐ pins to secure fabric
- ☐ strip fabric 36 x 8 ins. for bow

For Decoupage Box:
- ☐ fabric motifs
- ☐ fabric and batting for lining
- ☐ spray-on paint
- ☐ strip fabric twice circumference x 7 ins. for ruffle
- ☐ clear spray varnish

Fabric-covered Box

METHOD

1 Cut four lids each from fabric and batting, two from cardboard. Cut one strip of fabric and batting the circumference of base x twice depth of box. Cut one strip of fabric the circumference of lid x twice depth of lid, and one of batting with turn-under allowance only on one side.

2 Glue batting onto lid, gluing overlap allowances onto sides. Place batting side strip level with top of lid and glue around lid sides, taking overlap inside. Lightly hand-stitch to top lid piece. Trim cardboard lid liner to size. Cover with batting, turning and gluing overlap to back of cardboard. Set aside.

3 Cover box with batting as for lid. On outside, trim away depth of lid from batting at top. Glue edges. This is cut away to make lid fit better. Trim cardboard bottom liner to fit. Cover it with batting, turning and gluing overlap to back. Cover lid cardboard piece with fabric as for bottom cardboard piece, taking fabric overlap to back of cardboard and gluing or stitching to secure it in place.

4 Cover lid top with fabric, stitching allowances to batting on sides. Fold under ³/₄ in. along one long edge of lid side piece. Secure with small stitches or glue at folded edge, taking raw edge to inside. Glue to base. Glue lid cardboard liner into place. Repeat process for box, covering base, sides and inner sides with fabric. Glue cardboard liner into position.

5 Fold bow fabric over double, lengthwise, with right sides facing. Trim ends to an angle. Stitch around raw edges, leaving opening for turning. Trim corners, turn and iron. Tie bow and stitch on lid.

6 Glue braid around inside of box and lid to cover joins, if desired.

Decoupage Box

METHOD

1 Cover both pieces of cardboard with batting and fabric, following method for Fabric Covered Box. Set aside.

2 Paint box inside and out, except for inner bases of lid and box. Set aside to dry. Spray box with clear varnish, inside and out, to seal.

3 Fold in ¹/₂ in. on one short end of fabric strip and 2 ins. on each long side. Iron. Stitch a gathering thread along center, through all thicknesses. Draw up gathering to fit around inside base. Glue covered cardboard pieces in place inside box and lid. Glue ruffle in place inside box, overlapping raw edge with folded end.

4 Decoupage box using method for Baskets with Fabric Decoupage on page 73. Seal outside with clear varnish.

Say it with
Flowers

*B*ring *flowers into your home with these
beautiful fabric and painted blooms. This
crafty collection also includes an easily
constructed container for growing the real
thing, and some beautiful bunches to shape
a year-round fireplace screen.*

Down to DETAIL

Year Round Wreaths

Wreaths bring a welcome to any front door at any time of the year. They also look charming above a fireplace or dresser. If you use scented dried flowers, wreaths are a delightful addition to bathroom and bedroom.

Before You Begin

❏ Wreath bases can be made of many things including loops of garden vines; twisted straw bound with string; polystyrene floral rings; fabric tubes stuffed with synthetic stuffing; long strands of willow twisted together (the leaves will dry on strands) and thin strips of growing bamboo (again the leaves will dry on stems). What you choose will depend on your personal preference and the availability of raw materials. You can paint your base or leave it in its natural state – again this is a matter of personal preference. If you do decide to paint, spray paint is ideal.

❏ Add a loop of wire, ribbon or cord at the back for hanging your wreath.

❏ Just about anything pretty or unusual can be used to trim a wreath. Try using small and large dried flowers; dried pods; leaves; nuts; shells; purchased baubles; ribbons or fabric bows. Plastic fruit is also worth considering, especially if you paint it. It is a good idea to have all your trimmings assembled and ready for use (painted, trimmed, etc) before starting. Wire the trimmings into small bunches before attaching them to the base (as above). Other trimmings may be handled singly.

❏ Have a clear plan for your wreath before you begin constructing it. Take some time to experiment with colors, shapes and the distribution of the trimming. Concentrating the decorations at the lower end and adding some trailing ribbons can be very attractive.

❏ Make wreaths for Christmas, Easter and special birthdays – even make a wreath for a bride by drying her bouquet and fashioning a small wreath from it to preserve the memory forever.

MATERIALS
☐ materials for making base
☐ assorted trimmings
☐ glue gun
☐ lightweight floral wire
☐ optional spray paint

METHOD

1 Make base by twisting numerous strands or vines (or whatever you have chosen) around one another to form a pleasing shape. You can tuck in any loose ends or leave them to protrude.

2 Following your design, glue trimming around base with a glue gun.

3 Add ribbon bows, nuts, shells or any other suitable trimmings between decorations. Wire in hook for hanging.

Above: Wiring trimming into bunches
Left: Grape vine prunings twisted together to make rustic wreaths

Preserved Flowers

Preserved flowers and leaves present many charming opportunities for decorating.

Before You Begin

❏ Always pick perfect specimens for preserving. They are at their best in the mornings, just after the dew has dried. Be sure they are completely dry before beginning to treat them.

Drying Flowers with Borax

MATERIALS
- ☐ large, lidded plastic container
- ☐ quantity of borax
- ☐ small paintbrush
- ☐ sticky-tape
- ☐ clear spray varnish

METHOD

1 Pour a 1-in. layer of borax into container. Place flowers onto borax, keeping them separate from one another. Pour more borax around flowers, brushing it into crevices and folds until flowers are completely covered and there are no air pockets. Take care to retain shape of flowers.

2 Repeat layers until container is full. Replace lid and seal edges with sticky-tape. Leave for two weeks before checking on drying progress. Flowers may be left in borax until needed.

3 Remove borax from flowers with paintbrush before using. You can spray dried flowers with clear varnish.

Drying Leaves with Glycerine

MATERIALS
- ☐ firm leaves on small branches, such as beech; camellia; chestnut; hawthorn; eucalypts and aspidistras
- ☐ cooled mixture of one-third glycerine to two-thirds boiling water
- ☐ tall glass, narrow-necked containers

METHOD

1 Place approximately 3 ins. of cooled glycerine mixture into each jar. Crush ends of stems and place stem ends into jars to rest in mixture. Leave them in mixture until small droplets of glycerine appear on leaf surfaces.

2 Top up glycerine mixture occasionally if needed. Some leaves will turn brown, others take on decorative streaked effects.

Pressing Flowers

MATERIALS
- ☐ fresh flowers
- ☐ blotting paper
- ☐ heavy book (a telephone directory is ideal)
- ☐ scalpel or sharp craft knife

METHOD

1 If flowers have thick stems, pare away some thickness with a sharp craft knife or scalpel, allowing the stems to be pressed flat.

2 Place flowers onto two layers of blotting paper. Cover with another two layers of blotting paper and then place the flowers and blotting paper between pages of heavy book. Add extra weight, perhaps with a brick, and leave for several days before checking. Flowers are dry when they are papery to the touch.

Fireplace Screen

Bring spring into your home all year round! Take motifs from one of your floral furnishing fabrics or a wallpaper and make this lovely "basket of flowers" to sit in your fireplace when it's not in use. Brighten a dull corner with your lovely creation in spring and summer.

Before You Begin

❏ The size of this screen is entirely up to you. Choose the proportions that best suit your room and fireplace and use our photograph to help you decide.

❏ You will need a power jigsaw or a hand-held fretsaw to cut accurately around the motifs.

MATERIALS

- ☐ paper or fabric for pictures
- ☐ piece of ply, particle or craft wood of appropriate size and approximately ³⁄₄ in. thick
- ☐ two angle irons, at least 4 x 8 ins. for legs (larger sizes may be needed to support a very large screen)
- ☐ 1-in.-thick piece of timber at least 8 ins. square for support panel and to attach angle irons
- ☐ screws for brackets and support panel
- ☐ white glue
- ☐ acrylic paints
- ☐ power jigsaw or hand-held fretsaw
- ☐ small sharp scissors
- ☐ clear varnish

METHOD

Pattern Outline: ————————
See Pull Out Pattern Sheet at back of book.

1 Paint both sides of ply, particle or craft wood in same color as fabric background. Cut out flowers very precisely from paper or fabric and arrange them on the timber to suit size of screen, allowing sufficient space below for basket or urn. Sketch in basket or urn. Paint.

2 Using a paintbrush, coat back of flowers and their position on timber with glue. Place each flower into position, coating surface with glue again. Continue doing this until picture is built up.

3 When completely dry, cut carefully around outline of flowers and basket, leaving a ³⁄₄-in. margin. Paint edges. Glue and screw square of timber behind basket and screw on angle irons, just a little up from bottom edge so that screen tips slightly backwards. You may wish to paint the back of the screen and sign with the date of its making.

4 Seal entire screen with two coats of varnish.

Below left: Back view of Fireplace Screen
Below: Finished screen

Flower Picture

The six pretty floral motifs have been embroidered separately and then mounted and framed to create this delightful picture. The same embroideries could be used to make six miniature pictures.

Before You Begin

❏ The full-size drawings give the six floral motifs that were used – A wild orchid, B foxglove, C violets, D garlic, E primroses, F cowslip.

❏ The flowers have been worked in a variety of embroidery stitches which are clearly marked on the diagram for that piece.

MATERIALS
☐ Anchor Stranded Cotton, 1 skein each: White 01; Old Rose 075, 076, 077; Parma Violet 0109, 0110; Laurel Green 0208, 0211; Parrot Green 0254, 0256, 0258; Buttercup 0292, 0297; Gorse Yellow 0303
☐ 6 pieces cream, medium-weight embroidery fabric, each 10 x 10 ins.
☐ Milward International Range crewel needles no. 6 and no. 7
☐ tracing paper
☐ dressmaker's carbon paper

METHOD
See Pull Out Pattern Sheet at back of book for full-size drawings.

1 Trace each design from Pattern Sheet and transfer one to center of each fabric piece.

2 Work each design following stitch diagram and key on pages 84-85. All parts similar to numbered parts are worked in same color and stitch. Use no. 6 needle for 4-strand embroidery and no. 7 needle for 3-strand embroidery.

3 When stitching is complete, carefully iron all pieces, before having them professionally framed.

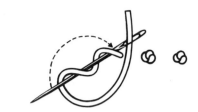

Figure 1

Figure 2

FRENCH KNOTS
1 Bring thread out at required position, hold thread down with left thumb and encircle thread twice with needle as shown (see Figure 1).
2 Still holding thread firmly, twist needle back to starting point and insert it close to where thread first emerged (see arrow). Pull thread through to back and secure it for a single French knot or pass on to position of next stitch as shown (see Figure 2).

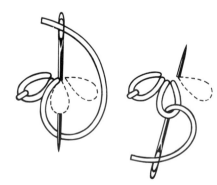

Figure 3   *Figure 4*

DAISY STITCH
1 Bring thread through at top and hold it down with left thumb. Insert needle where it last emerged and bring point out a short distance away. Pull thread through, keeping working thread under needle point as shown (see Figure 3).
2 Fasten each loop at foot with a small stitch (see Figure 4).

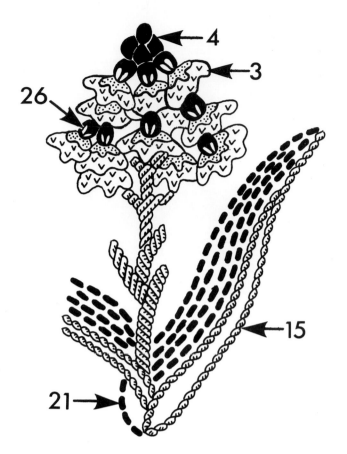

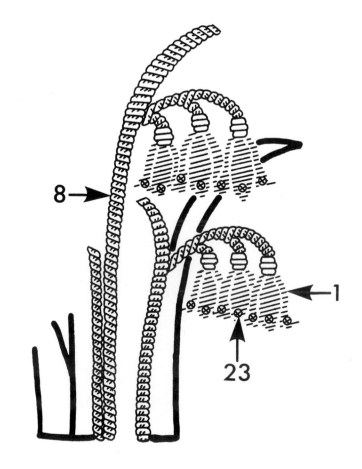

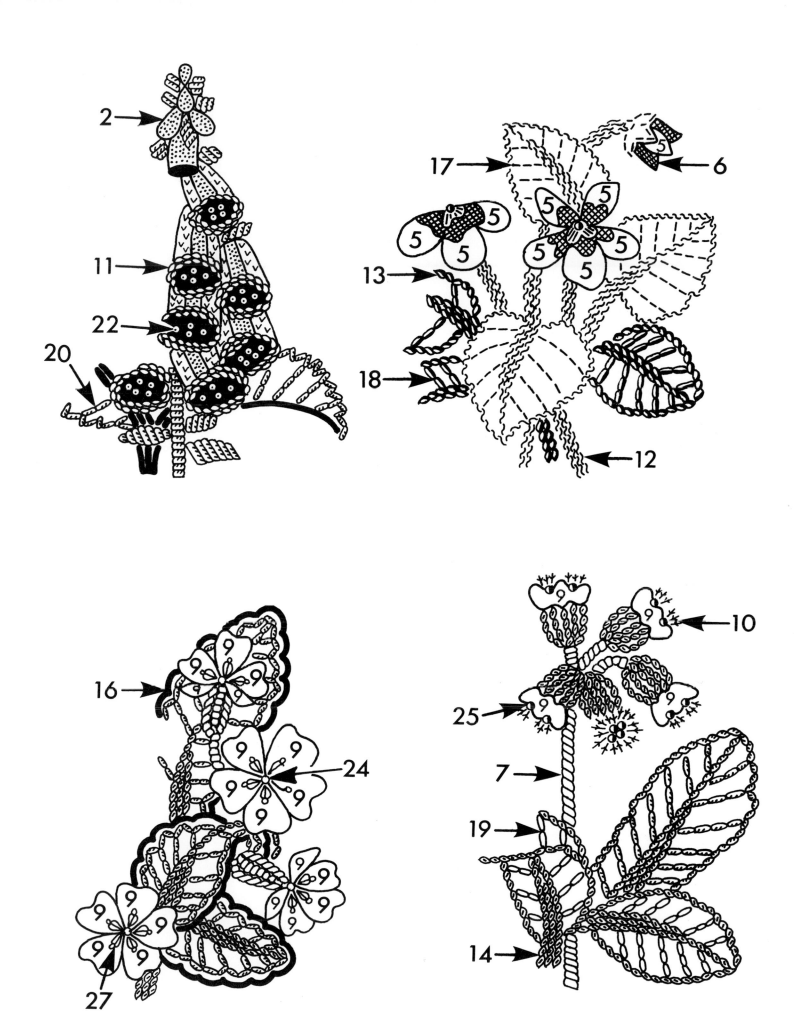

Fabric Flowers

Fabric flowers are an easy, inexpensive accessory. Made from fabric scraps, they will complete a coordinated color scheme. Make them small or large, and pile them into a lovely cane basket for a welcoming, country look.

Before You Begin

❏ The basis for these flowers is a simple gathered strip of fabric and the finished width of the flowers will depend on the width of the fabric.

MATERIALS

For each one-color flower:
☐ fabric strip approximately 20 x 6 ins. folded over double
☐ bamboo skewer
☐ craft glue or glue gun

For each two-color flower:
☐ two contrasting fabric strips each 20 x 4 ins.

☐ bamboo skewer
☐ craft glue or glue gun

METHOD

1 Fold one color strip over double, lengthwise, with wrong sides facing. For two-color flowers, place contrasting strips with right sides facing and stitch along one long side. Turn and iron open, then crease and iron along seam to fold in half. Curve short ends as shown.

2 Gather along raw edges of each folded strip. Draw up gathers. Beginning at one end, wind or fold fabric strip around end of skewer, gluing to secure as

Above left: Fabric Flowers
Above: Stitched and gathered strips

you go. Continue until all fabric is used, or desired size is achieved. Make flowers full and keep flower bottom flat.

3 Optional: To stiffen flowers, spray with laundry starch and dry thoroughly with a hair dryer.

Below: Rolling strips around skewer

No-sew Applique Pillow

If you don't sew, but love the look of applique you can create the same effect with bonding fabric, such as Vliesofix® or Stitch Witchery® and fabric paints, packaged in nozzled bottles, to fix and outline the motifs.

Before You Begin

❑ Wash all fabrics before using to remove sizing or chemical thickener coating the fibers. If you don't do this first, the sizing will wash out, taking the paint and applique with it.

MATERIALS

For pillow:
☐ 16-in.-square cotton fabric for front and two backs, each 16 x 9 ins.
☐ 2 yds. piping (optional)
☐ 12-in.-long zipper
☐ 3¹⁄₂ yds. ruffle in desired style (see page 42)
☐ 16-in.-square pillow form

For applique:
☐ cotton fabric to provide motif for applique
☐ 16-in.-length of paper-backed bonding fabric, such as Vliesofix or Stitch Witchery
☐ fabric paint
☐ scrap plain fabric 10 x 6 ins. for bow applique

METHOD

1 Cut out flower motifs with a ³⁄₄-in. border all around. Cut out bow like the one shown.

2 Place motif onto bonding fabric with glue side against back of motif. To bond, iron firmly on motif side. Cut around motif precisely. Motif has now absorbed adhesive. Peel away paper backing and position motif (or motifs) onto pillow front.

3 Iron motif onto pillow front, using an ironing cloth, if necessary, to protect fabric. It is sometimes easier to cut out exact shape of the motif in bonding fabric first, such as for bow, then bond as described above. Allow to cool.

4 Outline around all raw edges of motif, using paint and following manufacturer's instructions. Make a line of paint

that, when dry, seals edges of applique onto fabric. Allow paint to dry for 24 hours before making up pillow.

5 Make pillow as Ruffled Piped Pillow on page 40.

Above: Squeezing line of paint around bonded motif
Below: No-sew Applique Pillow

Down to DETAIL

Applique Pillows

If your machine can zigzag, you can applique beautiful motifs very easily. Think of applique as a way of painting a picture with fabric. Clothes, especially children's clothes, furnishings, table linen and bed clothes can all be made totally original with simple applique.

❏ Decide on your motif. Look for clear bunches of flowers or motifs that will be attractive as a feature.

❏ You may find you will have to strengthen the motif with iron-on interfacing if it is too flimsy. If interfacing is necessary, either cut out your motif and interface it or interface a piece of motif fabric and then cut it out. Alternatively, use the bonding fabric described in No-sew Applique on page 87.

❏ When using the following applique method, choose a sewing thread close to the color of the background fabric.

❏ Always use a new, sharp sewing machine sewing needle.

MATERIALS

☐ fabric featuring flowers, animals, borders or any motif that will lend itself to being cut out
☐ pillow front 16 x 16 ins., and two backs, each 16 x 9 ins. in fabric for pillow that matches perfectly with background of motif
☐ 2 yds. contrasting piping (see Down To Detail, page 42)
☐ 12-in.-long zipper
☐ 16-in.-square pillow form

METHOD

1 Cut out around motif, leaving ³/₄-in. margin all around.

2 Interface motif as desired, if necessary. Position motif on area to be appliqued. Pin or baste to secure.

3 Zigzag around motif ¹/₄ in. in from cut edge. Trim away excess fabric, close to stitching. Stitch again over first zigzag, using a slightly wider satin stitch.

4 When applique is complete, place piping around pillow front, with raw edges matching. Attach piping as instructed in Down To Detail on page 42.

5 Insert zipper as instructed in Down To Detail, page 42. Leaving zipper open, place back on front, with right sides facing. Stitch around outside edge, through all thicknesses, following stitchline for piping. Turn pillow to right side, place pillow form in cover, close zipper.

Far left: Finished Planter
Left: Inside Planter with base boards removed
Below left: Planter before painting

Versailles Planter

This wonderful timber planter box is in a classic style. It looks equally good on a balcony, patio or garden. If you plan to have it in the open, choose a water-resistant timber and seal it well.

Before You Begin

❏ Make a cardboard template the same size as the end of your support rails and mark accurately, in the middle of it, two drill holes for dowel insertion, 1 in. apart.

MATERIALS

☐ four corner posts, each 3 x 3 x 2½ ins. long; eight side rails, each 3 x ¾ x 17 ins. long; twenty-four side boards, each 3 x ¾ x 30 ins. long; two base supports, each 12 x 12 x 20 ins. long; six base boards, each 3 x ¾ x 17½ ins. long; thirty-two grooved dowel pieces, each ½ in. in diameter x 2 ins. long
☐ jigsaw or fretsaw for shaping
☐ screwdriver
☐ electric drill, ½-in.-diameter drill bit
☐ handsaw
☐ hammer
☐ plane or rasp
☐ marking square
☐ sandpaper
☐ wood glue
☐ sixty 1½-in. wood screws
☐ approximately 40-in.-square plastic sheet for lining

METHOD

1 Cut four corner posts to 2½ ins. long. Sand raw ends. Mark all four posts identically for insertion of dowels that will connect eight side rails to corner posts. Each side rail is held by four dowel pieces, two at each end.

2 Using your template, drill top dowel hole 3¼ ins. down and 1¼ ins. in from top of each corner post, with second ¾ in. away. These holes must be no more than 10 ins. deep. Drill lower pair of holes with same spacing 3¼ ins. up from bottom.

Using template, repeat holes on one other, adjoining side of each corner post.

3 Place six side boards butted together along a side rail to recheck for accurate length. Mark cutting edges and cut side rails. Sand raw ends, then using template, drill two dowel holes in each end of each side rail to align with holes drilled in corner posts. Spread dowel pieces with wood glue and insert into corner posts.

4 Check that remaining side boards are exactly 20 ins. long. Mark curved ends, using a cup or small saucer as a template. Cut to shape. Sand all raw edges.

5 Position six side boards over two side rails, with rails approximately 14 ins. apart. Note that bottoms of side boards should all be level and that side rails cover bottoms of vertical side boards. Check this distance with your drilled holes, as slight alterations may be necessary. Screw side boards to side rails, from inside.

6 Spread exposed dowel plugs in corner posts with glue. Attach side pieces to corner posts.

7 Mark ½ in. from top all around each corner post and ½ in. in from edges on top of post. With a saw, plane or rasp, cut off top edges at an angle using these lines as a guide. Cut from one line through post to the other, thus creating a 45° angle on each edge. Sand edges neatly.

8 Measure and cut two timber base supports. They should be same length as side rails. Screw each to lower inside edge of bottom side rails at base of opposite side boards. Cut base support boards to fit loosely across base, resting on these supports. The base boards are removable for ease of cleaning, painting or replacing water-damaged timbers, etc.

9 To allow planting directly into the box, tack plastic lining inside box. Be sure to have sufficient ease in plastic to allow for soil weight and remove base boards below where drainage holes are cut in plastic lining. Paint planter – if using oil paints, seal and undercoat it first.

Hand Towel

Applique this lovely apple blossom motif onto a purchased hand towel. To complete a pretty set, applique the same design onto a face washer.

MATERIALS

- ☐ Anchor Stranded Cotton, 1 skein each: Geranium 06; Carnation 023; Rose Pink 049; Grass Green 0240; Gorse Yellow 0302; Cinnamon 0368
- ☐ white hand towel, approximately 23 ins. wide
- ☐ 1 spool white Coats polyester sewing thread
- ☐ 1 piece each of fine cotton fabric to match thread shades 06, 023 and 049 for flowers, each 8 x 4 ins.
- ☐ 12 x 8 ins. fine cotton fabric to match thread shade 0240 for leaves
- ☐ 12 x 12 ins. iron-on interfacing
- ☐ colored crayons to match fabrics
- ☐ small piece of thin card for templates
- ☐ Milward International Range crewel needle no. 7

METHOD

1 Following cutting lines, carefully trace flower and leaf shapes and transfer tracings to thin card. Cut out templates.

2 Using templates, draw nine flowers and twelve leaves on iron-on interfacing. Color in with appropriate crayons. Cut out flowers and leaves.

3 With adhesive side down, arrange leaf shapes on pale green fabric, spacing them to allow a ¼-in. seam allowance all around. Iron each piece on to fabric and cut out with seam allowances.

4 Repeat step 3 for flowers, using three pink fabrics.

5 Clip all around into seam allowances of each piece. Turn seam allowances to wrong side. Baste turned edge in place, beginning and ending stitching on right side of fabric.

6 Arrange leaves and flowers on woven band of hand towel, overlapping leaves and flowers as shown in layout diagram.

7 Using three strands of floss throughout and taking care to keep back of work neat, work backstitch lines of different lengths in 0240, radiating outwards from flower centers. Work a French knot in 0302 at end of each line to represent stamens. Work veins of leaves in backstitch in 0240.

8 Using appropriately colored Anchor Stranded Cotton, work neat and evenly spaced blanket stitches around edges of all leaves and flowers, stitching through all thicknesses.

9 Using three strands of 0368, work gently curving chain stitches close together, between flowers to represent a thin branch.

10 Carefully remove all basting stitches. Press lightly.

BLANKET STITCH

1 Bring thread out on lower line, insert needle in position on upper line, taking a straight downward stitch with thread under needle point.

2 Pull up stitch to form a loop and repeat. Space stitches evenly (see Figure 1).

BACKSTITCH

1 Bring thread through on stitchline, then take a small backward stitch through fabric.

2 Bring needle through again a little in front of the first stitch, take another stitch, inserting needle at point where it first came through (see Figure 2).

CHAIN STITCH

1 Bring needle out at top of line and hold it down with left thumb.

2 Insert needle where it last emerged and bring point out a short distance away. Pull thread through, keeping working thread under needle point (see Figure 3).

FRENCH KNOTS

See page 82 for diagrams and instructions

Full-size Drawings

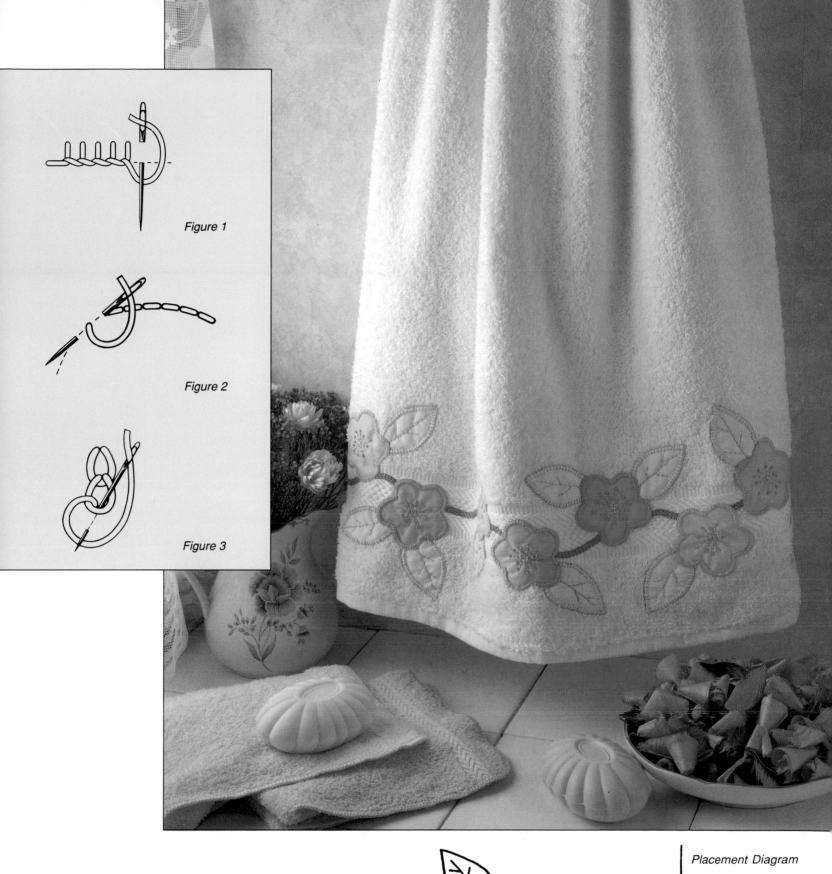

Figure 1

Figure 2

Figure 3

Placement Diagram

91

Floor *to* Ceiling

T ry these Clever Crafts for a quick transformation. Braid a rug for your floor, confidently create pillows, a circular cloth or a stenciled chair to match, spruce up your bathroom with a clever bathmat.

Braided Rug

Use up all your fabric scraps and leftovers to make this versatile floor rug. Folding and braiding joined strips of fabric make an economical and attractive floor covering.

Before You Begin

❏ Using fabric folders to prepare your fabric strips is not absolutely necessary but will make life a lot easier. These folders come in a kit from craft shops. They are slightly triangular in shape and funnel-like. The fabric strip is pulled through the folder and comes out with its edges folded to the center and the width of the strip is crushed to a usable size. If working without fabric folders, iron in both edges of fabric strips to meet in the middle. Crush slightly as you braid.

❏ For most fabrics, 5-6-in.-wide strips are ideal for braiding.

❏ Fabric requirements can vary enormously for different thicknesses, but as a rough estimate, 40 ins. of 45-in.-wide fabric will braid into a 12-in. square.

❏ Choose coordinating fabrics that blend well together and be sure to include a plain color for contrast. While you will be braiding with three lengths at a time, you can use more than three colors if you wish by joining lengths of different fabrics together.

If you use colors from your fabric scrap box, be sure to keep the variety spread throughout the rug and not allow banks of any one color to predominate.

❏ Always braid with three lengths – four becomes too difficult to manage. Weighting the already braided end while you work, allows you to pull gently and adjust as you go. You could jam the end in a drawer, tie it to some nearby object or have someone hold it for you. You will soon find your own tension and best method for coping with the bulk and the strips waiting to be braided. Some people find it easier to keep one of three strips shorter than the others.

MATERIALS
☐ fabric – generally cotton and wool types are best for floor coverings
☐ cotton twine for binding
☐ three fabric folders (if available)
☐ large, blunt flat-ended needle that may also curve at the end

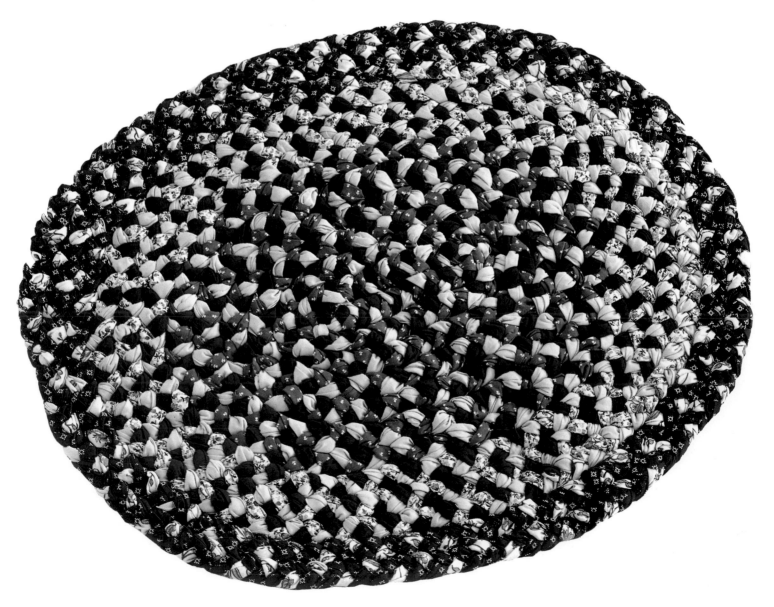

METHOD

1 Cut your strips and join them into continuous lengths by firmly machine stitching them, using a diagonal seam.

2 Prepare strips with fabric folders or by manually folding in the edges to the center of each strip and then folding them again until folded edges meet. Iron. Securely join three lengths together at one end and begin braiding. Continue braiding for approximately 40 ins. before sewing bands of braiding together.

3 Thread needle with twine and sew length of braiding together by taking needle between edge strip of braiding across to adjoining edge strip of next row (see diagram). Sew in such a way that braiding remains flat and strips butt up to each other. You may have to curve them slightly when the oval "end" of the rug is reached. The twine will show, but will not be a problem when the rug is complete.

4 Continue braiding and sewing until desired size of rug is achieved. Curve end of the braiding closely into edge of rug to secure – you may find it easier to cut away one or two strips to reduce bulk when end of the braid is sewn in. Secure all ends well.

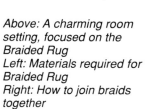

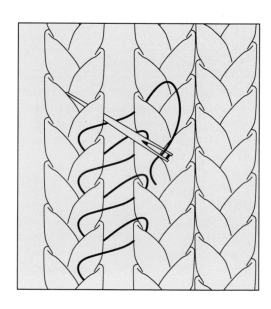

Above: A charming room setting, focused on the Braided Rug
Left: Materials required for Braided Rug
Right: How to join braids together

95

Bath Mat

This is a terrific solution to the perennial problem of soggy bath mats. An occasional scrub-down and an airing are all that are needed to keep it looking like new.

Before You Begin

❏ Decide what size mat you can accommodate in your bathroom before purchasing materials. Our mat measures 18 x 23 ins. Remember when you are deciding, that plastic tubing creates a 3/4-in. gap between each piece of timber.

MATERIALS

- ☐ ten lengths of dressed (planed) pine (PAR/DAR) 1 1/2 ins. wide x 3/4 in. deep x 18 ins. long
- ☐ 1 1/4 yds of 3/4-in.-diameter non-perishing plastic tube
- ☐ 2 1/4 yds. of 1/2-in.-diameter nylon rope
- ☐ electric drill with 3/4-in. and 1/2-in.-diameter drill bits

METHOD

1 Cut timber to size. Line up lengths side by side on their sides and rule a line 4 ins. from each end across all timber sides. Turn timber lengths over and repeat lines on other side for accurate drill positions. Find center of each side of timber pieces and mark this across ruled line.

2 Drill right through both side of each timber piece at center marking using small bit first, then drill through same hole with larger bit only to a depth of 3/4 in.

3 Cut plastic tubing into 2-in. lengths. These are used to separate timbers. Thread rope through timber and plastic tubes, starting at one end and working down one row of holes, out opposite end and back through remaining row of holes to other side. Knot ends securely. Hold knots over a lighted match to melt ends.

Plastic tubing linking boards

Stenciled Rug

These stenciled rugs are easily made with the creative use of masking tape to form a stencil. The instructions cover the general method and some tips for decorative options and methods.

Before You Begin

❏ Decide on your design before you start painting. It can be as complex as an all-over tartan pattern covering the whole rug, or a simple border of two lines around the perimeter of the rug. Practise on big sheets of paper until you get it just right. Whichever way you decide to proceed, make sure you prepare the simple equipment first, as it is difficult to alter patterns once you have started to paint.

❏ Use a sponge for coloring the rug. While paintbrushes are suitable, the results are not as even. Be adventurous with your use of color – often these rugs provide a way of tying together a previously difficult color scheme.

❏ Use acrylic, water-based paints. You can use the same paint as for your walls or even children's school paints. Oil paints can be messy and take too long to dry.

❏ Don't have too much paint on the sponge. Transfer some paint to a saucer – this allows you to scrape the sponge lightly across the saucer's edge to remove excess. Gently dab the paint in the areas to be colored – you will soon see how much pressure is necessary to create the effect you desire. The surface of the matting will prevent total absorption – another good reason not to have too much paint on the sponge as it could run off into spaces not sealed by tape and spoil your outline.

MATERIALS

☐ seagrass, coir or similar matting made from natural grasses
☐ masking tape of different widths
☐ acrylic paints
☐ small natural sponges
☐ rug-sized sheets of scrap paper for practising your patterns

Above right: Applying paint with a sponge
Right: Sticking down masking tape
Below: Stenciled Rug

METHOD

1 Choose a design. Press masking tape securely onto matting to outline it.

2 Completely fill in the areas to be colored with paint. Allow to dry thoroughly, then peel off masking tape.

3 You can paint over rug with a clear semi-gloss varnish to seal it but this is not absolutely necessary.

Table *tops*

*S*et the table and the scene so easily with your very own table linen. Choose coordinated fabrics and simply follow these steps to create decorative and useful placemats, napkins and circular cloths.

Circular Tablecloths

Circular tablecloths are a pretty disguise for unattractive items that need to be near by. There is no great mystery to making circular tablecloths. The secret lies in measuring and cutting accurately and then the sewing is just a straight line.

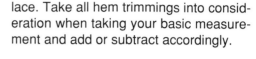
Before You Begin

❏ Measure from center of table, down to floor. Let's say this is 36 ins., just for this exercise. Add extra for hems if you plan to turn edge under rather than add a ruffle or

Left: Add flair to a plain cloth

lace. Take all hem trimmings into consideration when taking your basic measurement and add or subtract accordingly.

❏ Purchase four times this basic measurement of fabric plus 4 ins. unless your fabric is as wide as twice the basic measurement, or your table is very small.

MATERIALS
☐ sufficient fabric
☐ trims and ruffles as desired

METHOD

1 Join your fabric to make one large piece, large enough for circle (see Figure 1, page 101). To do this you will need to cut two pieces each twice basic length plus 4 ins. Leave one piece aside. Cut other piece down through middle, parallel with both selvages.

2 Join selvages of these cut pieces to selvages of large uncut piece (see Figure 1, page 101).

3 To cut out cloth, fold prepared fabric in half (see Figure 2, page 101). Fold in half again.

Left: Plain cloth topped with a square Overcloth
Below: Overcloth with bows covers the plain tablecloth

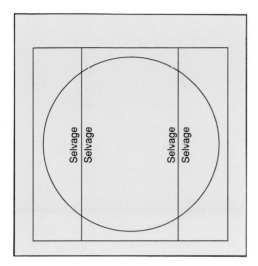

Figure 1

4 Place one end of tape measure at folded point and swing tape around, marking out arc of a circle, making a line at the basic measurement point. Cut through all thicknesses along this line.

5 To finish hem, measure around cloth circumference to determine quantities for ungathered lace or bias binding. Use at least one and a half times this measurement if gathering lace or a fabric ruffle. A simple hem can be finished by turning under $3/4$ in. on edge and stitching narrow cable cord into hem, using your sewing machine's zipper foot.

Overcloth

Before You Begin

❏ Plan how large you want the over-cloth to be. Make sure the proportion is right for your circular cloth.

Figure 2

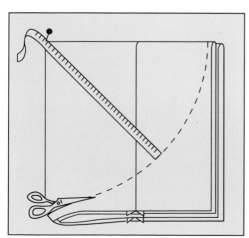

❏ Allow a minimum ruffle length of one and three-quarter times the outside edge of cloth. Strips of contrast or border fabric for ruffles can add a decorative note.

MATERIALS
☐ square of fabric for cloth
☐ strip of fabric for ruffle

METHOD

1 Join ruffle strips to make up required length. Gather one long edge. Turn over a narrow hem on other edge. Iron and stitch.

2 With right sides facing and raw edges matching, stitch ruffle around cloth. Neaten all raw edges with zigzag or over-locking. Remember to pleat ruffle slightly at corners to prevent it curling inwards.

Overcloth with Bows

MATERIALS
☐ circle of fabric – you may need to join fabric as instructed on page 100

☐ fabric strip for ruffle
☐ bias binding
☐ elastic

METHOD

1 Make ruffle and attach as for Step 1 of Overcloth.

2 At quarter points on circumference, stitch a casing from bias binding 1 in. wide x 3 ins. long. Thread elastic through casing making sure that outer end of elastic is sewn to casing at cloth edge. Leave top end of casing open. Stitch another length of elastic just above top of casing. Draw up elastic. Tie ends together to gather casing. Release elastic when washing and ironing cloth.

3 Using contrast or main fabric, cut lengths approximately 8 x 20 ins. Fold over double with right sides facing. Cut ends to a V. Sew around raw edges, leaving an opening for turning. Turn and iron. Tie into bows and sew securely to cloth, over gathering.

Tea Setting

Beautiful embroidery is a feature of this dainty linen afternoon tea set. Keep the shapes and other trims very simple to allow the detail of the embroidery to stand out.

Before You Begin

❑ The embroidery diagrams are full-size. Use the whole design for the tea cosy and the traycloth but only use the single flower below the dotted line for the napkin.

MATERIALS
- ☐ Anchor Stranded Cotton, 2 skeins each: Rose Pink 048, 050; Muscat Green 0279; 1 skein each: White 01; Rose Pink 052, 054; Muscat Green 0280; Antique Gold 0890
- ☐ 24 ins. of 45-in.-wide cream medium-weight embroidery fabric
- ☐ 12 ins. thick batting
- ☐ 12 ins. of 45-in.-wide cotton fabric for lining
- ☐ bias binding to match one color in Stranded Cotton
- ☐ Milward International Range crewel needle no. 7
- ☐ tracing paper
- ☐ dressmakers' carbon paper

METHOD
Cut following fabric pieces: one 14 x 12 ins. for tea cosy, one 20 x 14 ins. for traycloth and one 14 x 14 ins. for napkin.

Tea Cosy

Pattern Outline: — — — — — —
See Pull Out Pattern Sheet at back of book.

1 Trace off floral design and transfer it to center of one long side of one fabric rectangle, 2½ ins. from lower edge.

2 Work embroidery, following stitch diagram and key. All parts similar to numbered parts are worked in same color and stitch. When embroidery is complete, iron carefully on wrong side.

3 Trace tea cosy pattern from Pattern Sheet. Cut embroidered fabric to that shape. Cut two pieces of batting, two pieces of lining and one piece of fabric for back to same shape. Trim ¾ in. from all around batting pieces.

4 Baste batting to wrong side of embroidered piece and back. Baste lining over batting.

5 Place front and back together with lining sides facing. Bind curved edge of tea cosy, joining front to back as you go. Bind all around bottom edge in same way.

Traycloth

1 Trace off floral design and transfer it to fabric rectangle, 2 ins. from left-hand edge and 3 ins. from bottom edge.

2 Work embroidery, following stitch diagram and key. All parts similar to numbered parts are worked in same color and stitch. When embroidery is complete, iron carefully on wrong side. Bind edges of fabric rectangle, rounding off corners.

Napkin

1 Trace single flower and transfer it to lower left-hand corner of fabric square, 1½ ins. from both edges, omitting flower stem shown in solid black in stitch diagram.

2 Work embroidery, following stitch diagram and key. All parts similar to numbered parts are worked in same color and stitch. When embroidery is complete, iron carefully on wrong side.

3 Bind edges of fabric rectangle, carefully rounding off corners.

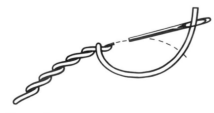

Figure 4

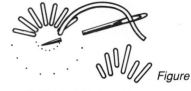

Figure 1

STRAIGHT STITCH
Single-spaced stitches are worked in either a regular or irregular manner (see Figure 1). Sometimes stitches vary in size.

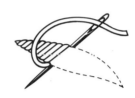

Figure 2

SATIN STITCH AND OPEN SATIN STITCH
For satin stitch, work straight stitches close together across shape (see Figure 2). Running stitch or straight stitch can be worked under satin stitch to form a padding and give a raised effect. Take care to keep a neat edge.

For open satin stitch, work stitches slightly wider apart and do not have padding underneath.

Figure 3

LONG AND SHORT STITCH
This is a form of satin stitch where stitches are of different lengths. It is often used to fill in a shape which is too large or too irregular to fill in with satin stitch. It can also be used to achieve a shaded effect.

For a first row, stitches are alternately long and short and closely follow shape outline. For a second row, stitches are worked to fit in for a smooth appearance (see Figure 3).

STEM STITCH
Work from left to right, taking small regular stitches along line of design. Thread always emerges on left side of previous stitch (see Figure 4).

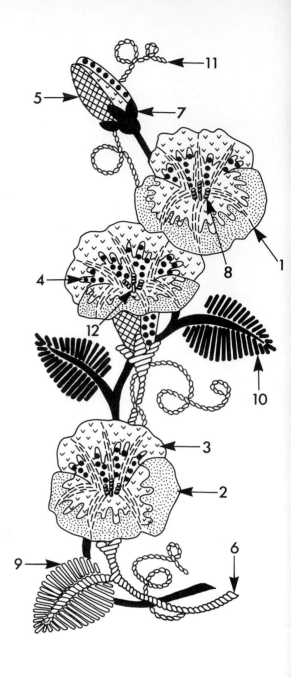

Full-size Drawing

KEY & STITCH GUIDE

Use three strands throughout

Long and short stitch:
1 01
2 048
3 050
4 052
5 054

Satin stitch:
6 0279
7 0280
8 0890

Open satin stitch:
9 0279
10 0280

Stem stitch:
11 0279

Straight stitch:
12 0890

Bindings *and* Borders

Today's fabrics provide wonderful opportunities for truly personalized household furnishings. You only have to wander through your local fabric shop to notice the ranges of coordinating and related fabrics available. Stripes to go with all-over florals, small prints to coordinate with florals, and perhaps another smaller floral to tie the whole thing together.

It's easy to be your own designer when coordinating these fabrics – use our examples for some inspiration. If no matching patterned fabrics are available, look at plains, small prints and stripes that match colors in other printed designs and develop your own

coordinated look. Providing the colors match, quite varied prints can look very effective when combined, especially if you sprinkle some plain bindings and fabrics amongst them.

Trims can work magic on plain fabrics too, and rows of stitched ribbons, braids and laces in a toning shade can make a simple, pillow cover into a wonderfully romantic decorating feature.

These coordinated looks are an attractive but expensive feature of some manufactured furnishings. You will see how easy it is to achieve these effects for yourself for very little cost and some planning and imagination.

Place Mats and Napkins

Nothing sets the scene quite like attractive table linen. These designs are delightfully easy to make, and adapt to all sorts of fabric designs. Choose cotton or polyester/cotton fabrics for easy care.

Place Mat with Self-fabric Border

MATERIALS
- ☐ main fabric 20 x 26 ins.
- ☐ fabric 14 x 20 ins. for center panel
- ☐ batting 17 x 23 ins.
- ☐ 1½ yds. bias binding or 1¼-in.-wide fabric strip, folded in half lengthwise

METHOD
Seam allowances of ½ in. allowed.

1 Center batting on wrong side of center panel. If desired, quilt through all thicknesses with intersecting, diagonal lines of stitching.

2 Baste center panel in center of main fabric piece with wrong sides facing, leaving a 3-in. border around panel. Turn under ½ in. on raw edges of main fabric piece and miter corners to give a 3-in. border. See diagram on page 107 for how to miter corners.

3 Turn border corners to right side. Tuck binding under folded edge, leaving ½ in. of binding protruding. Stitch folded edge down into place, stitching through all thicknesses.

Place Mat with Contrast Border

MATERIALS
- ☐ two pieces main fabric and one piece batting each 18 x 24 ins. long
- ☐ 2½ yds. contrast fabric border of your chosen width
- ☐ bias binding or 1¼-in.- wide strips fabric, folded in half lengthwise

METHOD
1 Place main fabric pieces with wrong sides facing and baste batting between them.

2 Cut two 18-in.-long and two 24-in.-long strips from border fabric. Turn under ½ in. on one long edge of each strip. Cut ends to perfect diagonals and join together with mitered corners.

3 With right sides facing and raw edges matching, stitch border to main piece. Trim corners. Turn and iron. Tuck binding under folded edge of border. Stitch folded edge down into place, stitching through all thicknesses.

Napkin with Contrast Border

MATERIALS

- □ square fabric 19 x 19 ins.
- □ four strips border fabric 9 x 3 ins. (vary width to suit fabric pattern)
- □ bias binding or 1¼-in.-wide strips fabric, folded in half lengthwise

METHOD

1 Turn under ½ in. along one long edge of each contrast border strip. Cut ends to perfect diagonals and join together with mitered corners.

2 Place border and square together so that right side of border faces wrong side of square. Stitch together around outside edge. Trim corners. Turn to right side and iron.

3 Tuck binding under folded edge of border. Stitch folded edge into place, through all thicknesses.

Napkin with Bias Trim

MATERIALS

- □ square fabric 19 x 19 ins.
- □ 2¼ yds. bias binding

METHOD

1 Press bias over double, lengthwise. Baste binding around edge of napkin, enclosing raw edge. Fold over one short end of bias. Overlap other raw edge at meeting point (see diagram).

2 Stitch through all thicknesses, being sure to catch both upper and lower edges of bias in seam.

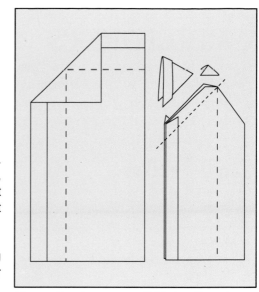

Above: How to sew a self-fabric mitered corner
Below: How to attach bias binding

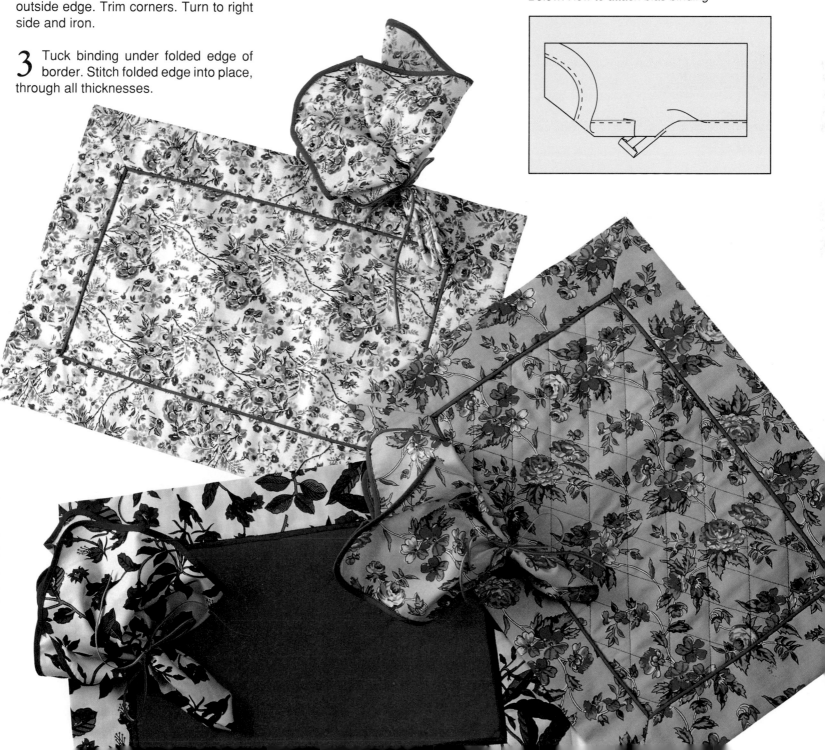

Centerpieces

There are many times when you need to decorate the center of your table, and often these occasions arise when there's nothing pretty in the garden. All you need is a little ingenuity.

Candles in Pots

MATERIALS
- ☐ small terra cotta pots, can be same size or various sizes
- ☐ wide-based candles to fit pots
- ☐ dried flowers
- ☐ ribbons
- ☐ silver foil
- ☐ sand to support candles and flowers, if needed

METHOD

1 If using sand, line base of pot with foil, place candle in pot and pour in sand. If not using sand, melt candle base slightly and place in pot, making sure it is secure.

2 Tuck bunches of dried flowers around base of candle.

3 Tie a bow around pot if desired. Place pots in a row down length of table or group them in center.

Christmas Centerpiece

Before You Begin

☐ Gather up all your materials before you begin and experiment with the design.

☐ A decorative option to consider is to spray the holly leaves gold prior to using. Dried oak leaves, real holly leaves or even plastic berry sprays look lovely tucked into the trimmings.

MATERIALS
- ☐ floral foam wreath
- ☐ fresh or artificial holly leaves
- ☐ staple gun or strong sewing pins
- ☐ bunches of ribbon, tied into bows
- ☐ several candles
- ☐ spray paint
- ☐ masking tape

METHOD

1 Cover wreath with masking tape, wrapping it as you would a bandage. Spray with gold paint and allow to dry.

2 Make indents for candles evenly around wreath with tips of scissors. Attach holly leaves around and down sides. Spray with gold paint. When paint is dry, push candles into indentations.

3 Tie bows from ribbon. Push pin through knot of ribbon. Pin ribbon bows in amongst holly.

Painted Fruit on a Silver Tray

MATERIALS
- [ ] assorted fruit and leaves
- [ ] silver tray
- [ ] gold spray paint

METHOD

1 Wash and dry fruit thoroughly, removing any dust and moisture.

2 Place fruit and leaves individually on newspaper and spray with gold paint. Allow to dry and spray again if required.

3 Arrange fruit decoratively on a silver tray. Tuck spare leaves into folded napkins for a special touch.

Fruit Centerpiece

MATERIALS
- [ ] cone-shaped floral base
- [ ] conifer or holly cuttings
- [ ] red apples
- [ ] metal meat skewers
- [ ] suitable tray

METHOD

1 Push one end of skewers through cone and push apples onto other end. Use as many skewers as you need to form a pleasing arrangement.

2 Tuck holly and conifer cuttings around apples. Place arrangement on the tray.

New Looks for Old

One of the best low-cost decorating tricks around is to conceal shabby items with generous amounts of inexpensive fabric. It's easy to do, takes a little time and patience, but the results are wonderful and well worth the effort. Try some of these ideas for yourself and soon you'll be wanting to cover everything in sight!

Fabric-covered Chair

METHOD

You don't need a pattern to cover that old director's chair with fabric. It's a breeze if you follow these simple instructions.

1 Join lengths of your chosen fabric to make a large square. Practise on a double bed sheet to see what size square you will need. You may have to join fabric at selvages to achieve the correct area of fabric. Iron seams open.

2 Open out square and place it over chair, pushing it into corners and bundling it up around bases of arms and into seat area. Pin to secure while this fitting process is carried out. Once you are satisfied with fit and drape, mark positions of eight buttonholes, one either side of arm bases, at front, and again at back.

Top right: Detail of bow
Right: Give new life to some well-loved, old pieces for a cheap redecorating idea
Below: Chair before covering

3 Remove fabric and make 1¼-in.-long buttonholes as marked. Replace fabric on chair. Tie string through buttonholes to secure. Trim around base at floor level, to create even length. Remove fabric from chair and hem lower edge as marked or fold edge over cable cord and stitch down with zipper foot of your machine.

4 Make ties from scrap fabric, cut away from hem, or face them with a pretty, contrasting fabric as we have done. Cut strips about 9 x 40 ins. Fold double, lengthwise, with right sides facing. Sew around all edges leaving an opening for turning. Turn and iron. Insert ties through buttonholes and tie into bows at base of arms and back of chair.

5 Make a ruffled pillow for comfort as well as good looks! Cut out two pieces of contrast fabric, the same size as chair seat plus seam allowances, and sufficient ruffle plus seam allowances. Make cover in same way as Ruffled Piped Pillow on page 40. Instead of a pillow form, baste several layers of batting together around edges and place inside cover.

Above: Trimming hem of chair cover
Below: Fabric-covered Boxes

Boxes

METHOD

These sturdy storage boxes are recycled cardboard cartons cut to a new size and shape and covered with decorative fabric.

1 Use spray-on adhesive, white glue, or a glue gun to cover the boxes. Remember to allow sufficient fabric at edges to tuck under and glue securely.

2 Cover cardboard completely with fabric for a professional result.

Footstool

Footstool

METHOD

You'll never believe this but under this glamorous footstool is an orange crate from the market!

1 Cut a foam-rubber base for top and cover with fabric, pulling it down tightly at corners and edges. Secure with a staple gun or small tacks. Cut away excess fabric below staples.

2 Use selvage of fabric as bottom hem. Form a deep box pleat at each corner, staple fabric around box, placing staples beside first row, securing top cover. Trim away excess fabric close to staples.

3 Cover staple rows with a band of fabric, leaving tails at each corner.

4 Tie tails into bows. You need not sew these ties. Simply iron under raw edges and fold tie over double, lengthwise, to hide all raw edges.

Notice Board

METHOD

An old frame that has been covered with fabric makes a super notice board.

1 Cover a piece of cork with fabric. Glue a contrasting fabric all over an old wooden picture frame.

2 Insert cork into frame. Secure it with tacks as you would a picture. Attach a wire or hook for hanging.

Storage Cans

METHOD

These are useful for storing kitchen utensils, pencils on desks or even flowers.

1 Cut a strip of fabric long enough to go around the can plus ¾ in. for over and underlap x height of can plus 2 ins. to fold over the rim to the inside. You can finish your fabric under the rim if you prefer.

2 Cover empty, clean food cans with craft glue. Glue strip around can.

Above: Notice Board
Below: Storage Cans

Index